Grant William Shull

# BE-A-PEACEMAKER.COM

FOREVER: The Peacemaker's Manifesto of The Agility of Grace

*SO THAT …*
*YOU May Become The Infinity of Happiness*
*YOU Were Always Meant To Be &*
*BE A CHILD OF GOD…*
*FOREVER!*

© 2019 Grant William Shull

## TABLE OF CONTENTS

| | |
|---|---|
| TABLE OF CONTENTS | 2 |
| The Dedication of The Peacemaker | 5 |
| *To Elizabeth, My First Wife…* | 5 |
| The Vision of The Peacemaker | 6 |
| *BE-A-PEACEMAKER.COM – SEEK LOVE* | 6 |
| The Unity of The Peacemaker | 7 |
| The Mission of The Peacemaker | 9 |
| *BE-A-PEACEMAKER.COM – SERVE MERCY* | 9 |
| The Goal of The Peacemaker | 10 |
| *BE-A-PEACEMAKER.COM -- WAGE PEACE* | 10 |
| The Tautology of The Peacemaker | 11 |
| *BE-A-PEACEMAKER.COM. – BE FOREVER* | 11 |
| The Way of the Peacemaker | 12 |
| *Teach Your Children Well – Forever* | 12 |
| The Purpose of The Peacemaker | 14 |
| *TO BE FOREVER: BE-A-PEACEMAKER.COM* | 14 |
| The Shrewdness of The Peacemaker | 15 |
| *Give Away What You DO NOT OWN To Possess What You CANNOT BUY* | 15 |
| The Call of The Peacemaker | 18 |
| *FOREVER! BE-A-PEACEMAKER.COM* | 18 |
| The Creed of The Peacemaker – Transilluminated | 19 |
| The Creed of the Peacemaker – Standard Form | 21 |
| The Journey of The Peacemaker – Poems to Light the Path | 22 |
| *Another Word for Sky* | 22 |
| *Psalm 23 – A Poem of David, A Peacemaker* | 22 |
| *A Trilogy of Poems by A Journeyman Peacemaker* | 22 |
| The Prayer of The Peacemaker | 23 |
| *FOREVER* | 23 |
| The Meditation of The Peacemaker | 27 |
| The Profession of the Peacemaker | 31 |

| | |
|---|---|
| *The Dignity of Tikkun Olam* | 31 |
| *The Mercy of Abram to Preserve The Dignity of Sodom* | 32 |
| *Genesis 13:13-15:6 (DRA)* | 33 |
| The Sermon for The Peacemaker | 34 |
| *Matthew Chapters 5-7 (DRA)* | 34 |
| The Judgement of The Peacemaker | 39 |
| *Be a Sheep: Matthew Chapters 24-25 (DRA)* | 39 |
| The Practice of The Peacemaker – Dignity at Work | 44 |
| *The Agility of Grace* | 44 |
| *Allowing The Transfiguration to Happen -- The Kingdom Come* | 46 |
| *MERCY is BOTH the KEY, and THE ENTIRE SUBSTANCE of THE KINGDOM OF HEAVEN.* | 46 |
| *Trusting The Agility of Grace – Make Your Work Child's Play Again* | 47 |
| *Therefore, Let Us Be Resolved:* | 58 |
| The Tools & Texts of The Peacemaker | 60 |
| *Starter List* | 60 |
| *The Pattern of A Peacemaker* | 65 |
| *AND THAT'S NOT ALL* | 70 |
| The Dignity of The Peacemaker | 71 |
| The Question of the Peacemaker | 72 |
| *Do I Have to be of The Catholic Faith Tradition to Be a Peacemaker?* | 72 |
| The Plowshare of The Peacemaker | 83 |
| *The Rosary of Agility* | 83 |
| The Commission of The Peacemaker | 88 |
| *Matthew 28:18-20 (DRA)* | 88 |
| The Hope of The Peacemaker | 89 |
| *To Overcome The FUDS of OPML & To Rest with Perfect Peace* | 89 |
| The Invitation of The Peacemaker | 90 |
| *To Party for Mercy's Sake Like Never Before* | 90 |
| *Come… Come… Come… LET US PARTY!* | 90 |
| *Let Us Take The Water of Life…* | 90 |
| *Freely…* | 90 |
| *BE-A-PEACEMAKER.COM* | 90 |
| *FOREVER!* | 90 |
| The Resolution of The Peacemaker | 91 |

| | |
|---|---|
| *Therefore, Let Us Be Resolved:* | 91 |
| *Because:* | 91 |
| *Your Eternal Life &* | 91 |
| *Our Ultimate Happiness* | 91 |
| *Literally Depend on This…* | 91 |

## The Haiku of The Peacemaker – The Sending Forth — 93

*Namaste! Seek Love;* — 93
*Serve Mercy: Send Happiness;* — 93
*Wage Peace: NAMASTE!* — 93

## The Beginning of the Peacemaker — 94

HERE ENDS YOUR SEARCH — 94
FOR THE BEGINNING — 94
OF YOUR — 94
FOREVER… — 94
BE-A-PEACEMAKER.COM — 94
AND BE ONE — 94
WITH… — 94
FOREVER! — 94

## The Dreams of the Peacemaker — 95

IMPACT — 95
As _____, a _____, I want to be able to deliver _____ to my Waiting & Thirsty Neighbors, so that _____! — 95
CONTRIBUTION — 96
As _____, a _____, I want to be able to _____, so that _____! — 96
ENGAGEMENT — 97
As _____, a _____, I want to be able to _____ with _____, a _____ so that _____! — 97
DATA POINT — 98
As _____, a _____, when I _____, I want to be able to sense _____ with my _____ in the form of _____, so that _____! — 98
TRANSCEND THAT BLOCKER – NAME IT & TAME IT — 99
As _____, a _____, I am not able to _____ because _____! — 99

## The Notes of the Peacemaker — 100

*Write About What You Know…* — 100

# The Dedication of The Peacemaker

August 27, 2019

## To Elizabeth, My First Wife…

Whose shoulder I now fondly & virtually poke in This Celebration of The Day of Her Birth as I wish her many happy returns of The Day for many, many years to come.

Surely, she IS BOTH her "Uncle" Henry's niece, AND my **FOREVER** Spiritual Harbinger, for had she not divorced me, and made me to be Her Neighbor, I never honestly would have been made to GO BTFI, I never fully would have been made to put on my Amazing Technicolor Dream Coat fashioned by The Agility of Grace in ALL of His Shekinah Glory, and I never truly would have been made to learn The Way of The Peacemaker.

Indeed, I never, ever would have been made to create BE-A-PEACEMAKER.COM as the realization of her graceful, persistent, catechismal dream.

Dream On in Goodwill, My Forever Love… That we may dance The Dance of Eternal Friendship, and sing The Song of Divine Mercy together with The Saints, and with Angels and Archangels, and with ALL The Company of Heaven as we Party for Mercy's Sake as Always Like Never Before, Always in Divine Intercourse with Our LORD God Elohim, Always in The Ineffable Light of Glory, Always in The Divine Now, and Always with Each Other, even as we are made to be ONE by His Grace in…

***FOREVER!***

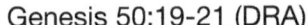

Genesis 50:19-21 (DRA)

The Vision of The Peacemaker

BE-A-PEACEMAKER.COM – *SEEK LOVE*

To Make Our World a Better, Brighter Place for ALL OF US to live in & to love in, each & every day…

AND… To Sing Along with MY HEART:

TAKE ACTION! ➡ FOREVER!

Wouldn't you be,
Couldn't you be,

(Thank YOU, Mr. Rogers)

TIKKUN OLAM
WITH…THE AGILITY
MERCIPALOOZA! OF GRACE
YES!

How Fascinating!
NO FEAR  Mercy  NO Reprisals

Please…
Won't you be
My Neighbor?

Won't you… JOIN: The Little Mustard Seed *MERCIPALOOZA FOREVER CORP* COME
COME! ➡ BE-A-PEACEMAKER.COM HOME!

…**FOREVER**!

## The Unity of The Peacemaker

A note to my gentle readers, and seekers of a productive peace who may be reading this for commercial purposes ...

I do not divide the world into the unproductive, ineffective, and inefficient categories of *the religious* and *the secular*, or *the commercial* and *the spiritual*.

And neither does the Agility of Grace.

If you undertake to BE-A-PEACEMAKER.COM, then you'll find that Agility is one single ethos arising from your core self that allows you to think outside-the-box in every area of your life. In fact, the Agility of Grace may be found at the heart of every healthy major religion on the face of the planet calling each, and everyone of us Home to Mercy each, and every day.

From the Catholic faith tradition, which is the modern-day extension of the Messianic Faith Tradition that runs all the way back to Eden, and all the way forward past to the present day to The Wedding Feast at the End of Time, we find the truth that *Mercy Endures Forever*, and that he, above all people, places and things, indeed, above all else, is the most valuable of any, and of all. Therefore we must comb The Agility of Grace from all of the best practices of the world's ideologies, methodologies, whatever-have-you-ologies, religions, and non-religions, and add the solid-as-a-rock practices of Merciful Living as the cherry on the top. We must be diligent to do this always, so that we might maximize the creative promise for each, and every person on each, and every delivery team they are part of, regardless of the type of product they may be striving to deliver to there waiting, and thirsty neighbors.

I do not differentiate, because what is good for the spirit is always good for edifying commerce, and what commerce is good for edifying my neighbor is always good for the spirit.

The only things I ask us all to bear in mind in all cases is that:

- *People are the secret ingredients in any formula for success*
- *Mercy is the key to everything*
- *Putting the focus on money is alway the harbinger of less than nothing at all, and*
- *Progress toward Our Ultimate Happiness of Divine Intercourse Together in* **Forever** *is always The Ultimate Goal of The Agility of Grace.*

And for all of my readers who have come here for guidance on team-based creative productivity enhancement with regard to non-commercial purposes…

As long as you do not mix your motives with the madness of monetary gain for its own sake, you should be OK.

Certainly, make all the money you can with whatever you deliver to promote Happiness among our Neighbors, and remember to reinvest the money you do make toward the merciful purpose for which you formed your enterprise in the first place.

Then, Just keep on keepin' on with The Agility of Grace as your guide…
**FOREVER!**

# The Mission of The Peacemaker

BE-A-PEACEMAKER.COM – *SERVE MERCY*

To Do More Better, Even More Better with The Agility of Grace Each & Every Day…

***FOREVER!***

# The Goal of The Peacemaker

## BE-A-PEACEMAKER.COM -- *WAGE PEACE*

SO THAT WE SHALL Party for Mercy's Sake as Always Like Never Before in The Ineffable Light of The Glory of His Grace by Engaging Always Like Never Before in The Everlasting Ecstasy of Divine Intercourse with Elohim, Our Eternal Community of The Creative Golden Promise of Love, and with Our Likewise Mercifully Partying Neighbors as We Always Come Together in the Never-ending Bliss of our Eternal Home of Peace where we Always Become Always Like Never Before…

***FOREVER*!**

# The Tautology of The Peacemaker

**BE-A-PEACEMAKER.COM. – *BE FOREVER***

BY THE AGILITY OF GRACE
BE MERCY AND BE MERCY
BE MARY, AND BE MERRY
BE *FOREVER*
AND
BE…
*FOREVER*.

BECAUSE A CHILD OF *FOREVER*
IS ALSO…
*FOREVER*.

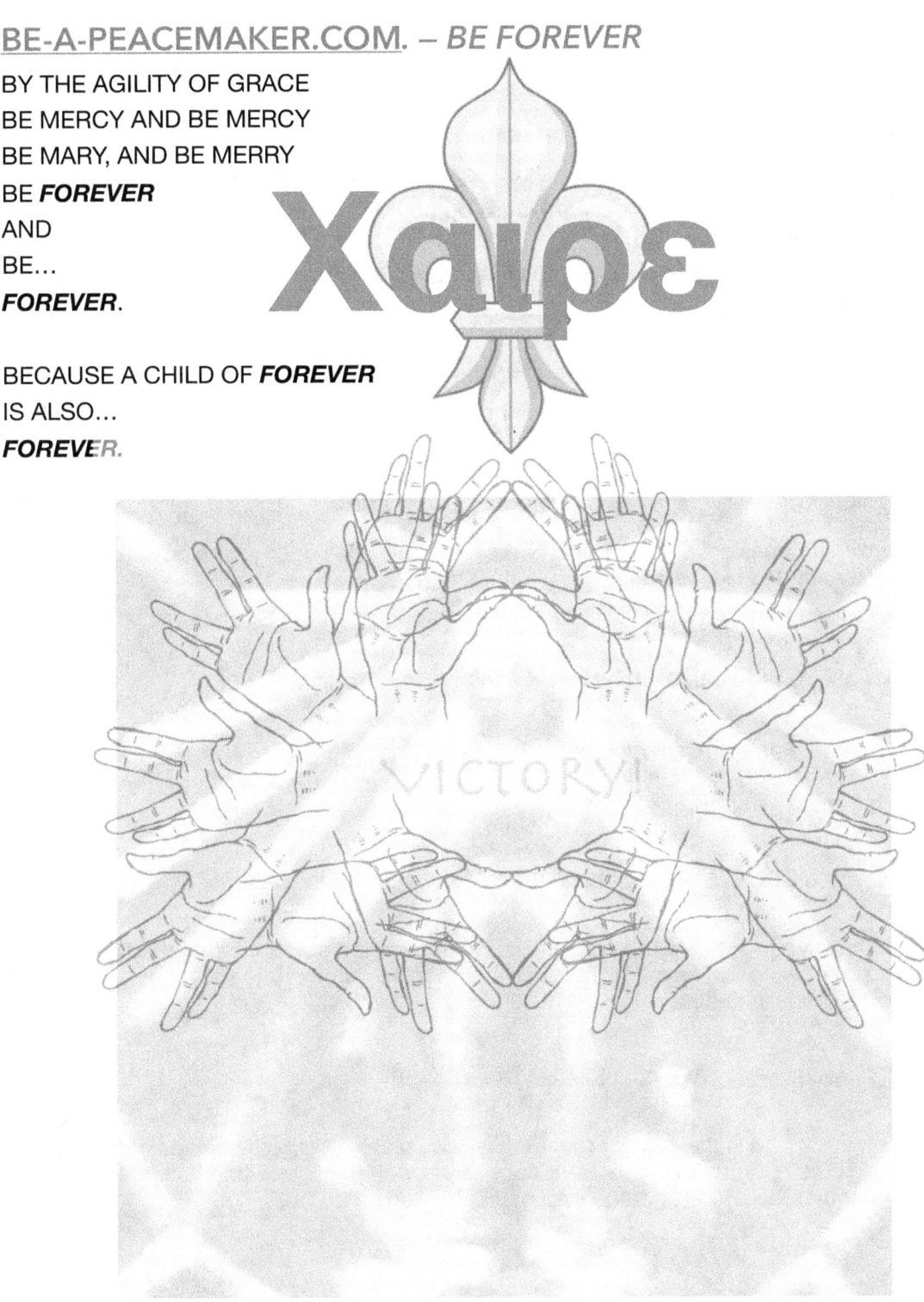

# The Way of the Peacemaker

## Teach Your Children Well – *Forever*

### Psalm 46 [Psalm 45 (DRA)]

**1** Unto the end, for the sons of Core, for the hidden.

**2** Our God is our refuge and strength: a helper in troubles, which have found us exceedingly.

**3** Therefore we will not fear, when the earth shall be troubled; and the mountains shall be removed into the heart of the sea.

**4** Their waters roared and were troubled: the mountains were troubled with his strength.

**5** The stream of the river maketh the city of God joyful: the most High hath sanctified his own tabernacle.

**6** God is in the midst thereof, it shall not be moved: God will help it in the morning early.

**7** Nations were troubled, and kingdoms were bowed down: he uttered his voice, the earth trembled.

**8** The Lord of armies is with us: the God of Jacob is our protector.

**9** Come and behold ye the works of the Lord: what wonders he hath done upon earth,

**10** Making wars to cease even to the end of the earth. He shall destroy the bow, and break the weapons: and the shield he shall burn in the fire.

**11** Be still and see that I am God; I will be exalted among the nations, and I will be exalted in the earth.

**12** The Lord of armies is with us: the God of Jacob is our protector.

And with this I offer an excellent meditation on the surprisingly, and excruciatingly soul crushing, and exhaustingly brow dampening call to ACTION required by the verb rendered into English from the Hebrew as "be still"…

https://www.hebrew4christians.com/Meditations/Be_Still/be_still.html

…may you make your peace with Chapter 2 of St. James' letter in the cross-reading of this excellent piece of exegesis as an excellent co-companion summary to the readings from the Twenty-First Sunday in Ordinary time 2019…

http://www.usccb.org/bible/readings/082519.cfm

With many thanks, and sincere intent that Elohim may bless all of his Gestures of Stillness, I celebrate this offering from Mr. John J. Parsons made with the Grace that is at the heart of his name, and the Peace that is at the soul of his mission.

May we all exult Elohim as we pursue His Peace THROUGH our graceful, persistent ACTIONS with all of our heart, and with all of our soul, and with all of our strength, and with all of our mind, as we learn to joyfully love our Neighbors as ourselves in MERCIPALOOZA!

With veneration for Our Most Blessed Ever-Virgin Mother, Kecharitomene, The Queen of Grace, and with great respect for all of the deeply mindful, honorable, engaging, hard-working women who have ever learned, who now are learning, and who shall ever learn how to be ever-more perfectly human, and ever-more slightly Divine by striving always to BE THE CHANGE they want to SEE in the world at Agnes Scott College, especially my daughter Cait, who has consistently chosen to live her life with honor, and to blaze *A Worthy Path of Peace* that all of her younger sisters might emulate according to their own particular whimsy, and with their own particular *fromage.*

In the honor of all of these most honorable human souls, who have helped to teach this parent well, I present to you my *less-than-original*, though deeply held conviction that our best way forward, both in every moment of The Divine Now, and even at the hour of our death is:

- *To think deeply, act honorably, and engage practically, positively, and progressively with The Agility of Grace for Mercy's Sake like Never Before as we strive together to resolve the most pressing issues of Our Zeitgeist, so that, we shall overcome the FUDS of OPML thinking, and be able to make Our World a Better, Brighter Place to Live In, and to Love In as We Do More Better, Even More Better, Each & Every Day until…***FOREVER.***

And I invite YOU, my dear reader, to join me in the making our own peculiar communal "Cheese of Whimsy" together by reading the pages that follow, taking their meaning to heart, and joining both with me, and with all who strive honorably for PEACE THROUGH ACTION in the hope of realizing Our Ultimate Happiness of Tranquility in our lifetime. Indeed, I invite you to:

BE-A-PEACEMAKER.COM

And to become a member of The Little Mustard Seed *MERCIPALOOZA FOREVER CORP…*

**FOREVER**!

## The Purpose of The Peacemaker

## TO BE *FOREVER:* BE-A-PEACEMAKER.COM

**IT IS MY PURPOSE** as **GRANT WILLIAM SHULL**
A Journeyman Peacemaker & Certified Agile Leader
**TO INVITE YOU & EVERYONE I MEET**
**TO BE-A-PEACEMAKER.COM**...

**SO THAT YOU MAY BE**
**THE INFINITY OF HAPPINESS**
**YOU WERE ALWAYS MEANT TO BE...**
**FOREVER!**

*SO THAT YOU MAY BE THE HAPPINESS YOU SEEK...*
**FOREVER!**

SO THAT YOU MAY BE THE MERCY YOU SERVE
In Living & Dancing & Singing in *THE DIVINE NOW* with The Agility of Grace...
**FOREVER!**

*SO THAT YOU MAY BE THE AGILITY OF GRACE YOU SEEK*
By engaging the people of This Earth with ALL of the advantages of The Machine-Platform-Crowd Delivery Age through well-intentioned work with The Church, which IS The Happiness of Eucharistic Living for the Goodwill of ALL of Your Neighbors...
**FOREVER!**

SO THAT WE, WITH THE GENTLE GUIDANCE OF THE AGILITY OF GRACE may find Our Ultimate Happiness & Be Found Worthy & Be Called "Children of God" In The Divine Now...
**FOREVER!**

SO THAT WE MAY LEARN TO PARTY FOR MERCY'S SAKE Like Never Before as we learn to work together through MERCIPALOOZA.com...
**FOREVER!**

TO DO MORE BETTER TO BE MORE BETTER, EVEN MORE BETTER Each & Every Day Of Our Existence...
**FOREVER!**

# The Shrewdness of The Peacemaker

## Give Away What You DO NOT OWN To Possess What You CANNOT BUY

We shall let that stand mostly on its own with just two additional thoughts, and a pair of strange stories Jesus told in sequence about STUFF from **Luke 16 (DRA)**.

Remember, due to the Bite of Eden:
- You neither OWN, nor DESERVE anything you have, AND
- You can neither earn, nor buy neither MERCY, nor **FOREVER** at any price.

### Luke 16 (DRA)

**1** And he said also to his disciples: There was a certain rich man who had a steward: and the same was accused unto him, that he had wasted his goods.

**2** And he called him, and said to him: How is it that I hear this of thee? give an account of thy stewardship: for now thou canst be steward no longer.

**3** And the steward said within himself: What shall I do, because my lord taketh away from me the stewardship? To dig I am not able; to beg I am ashamed.

**4** I know what I will do, that when I shall be removed from the stewardship, they may receive me into their houses.

**5** Therefore calling together every one of his lord's debtors, he said to the first: How much dost thou owe my lord?

**6** But he said: An hundred barrels of oil. And he said to him: Take thy bill and sit down quickly, and write fifty.

**7** Then he said to another: And how much dost thou owe? Who said: An hundred quarters of wheat. He said to him: Take thy bill, and write eighty.

**8** And the lord commended the unjust steward, forasmuch as he had done wisely: for the children of this world are wiser in their generation than the children of light.

**9** And I say to you: Make unto you friends of the mammon of iniquity; that when you shall fail, they may receive you into everlasting dwellings.

**10** He that is faithful in that which is least, is faithful also in that which is greater: and he that is unjust in that which is little, is unjust also in that which is greater.

**11** If then you have not been faithful in the unjust mammon; who will trust you with that which is the true?

**12** And if you have not been faithful in that which is another's; who will give you that which is your own?

**13** No servant can serve two masters: for either he will hate the one, and love the other; or he will hold to the one, and despise the other. You cannot serve God and mammon.

**14** Now the Pharisees, who were covetous, heard all these things: and they derided him.

**15** And he said to them: You are they who justify yourselves before men, but God knoweth your hearts; for that which is high to men, is an abomination before God.

**16** The law and the prophets were until John; from that time the kingdom of God is preached, and every one useth violence towards it.

**17** And it is easier for heaven and earth to pass, than one tittle of the law to fall.

**18** Every one that putteth away his wife, and marrieth another, committeth adultery: and he that marrieth her that is put away from her husband, committeth adultery.

**19** There was a certain rich man, who was clothed in purple and fine linen; and feasted sumptuously every day.

**20** And there was a certain beggar, named Lazarus, who lay at his gate, full of sores,

**21** Desiring to be filled with the crumbs that fell from the rich man's table, and no one did give him; moreover the dogs came, and licked his sores.

**22** And it came to pass, that the beggar died, and was carried by the angels into Abraham's bosom. And the rich man also died: and he was buried in hell.

**23** And lifting up his eyes when he was in torments, he saw Abraham afar off, and Lazarus in his bosom:

**24** And he cried, and said: Father Abraham, have mercy on me, and send Lazarus, that he may dip the tip of his finger in water, to cool my tongue: for I am tormented in this flame.

**25** And Abraham said to him: Son, remember that thou didst receive good things in thy lifetime, and likewise Lazareth evil things, but now he is comforted; and thou art tormented.

**26** And besides all this, between us and you, there is fixed a great chaos: so that they who would pass from hence to you, cannot, nor from thence come hither.

**27** And he said: Then, father, I beseech thee, that thou wouldst send him to my father's house, for I have five brethren,

**28** That he may testify unto them, lest they also come into this place of torments.

**29** And Abraham said to him: They have Moses and the prophets; let them hear them.

**30** But he said: No, father Abraham: but if one went to them from the dead, they will do penance.

**31** And he said to him: If they hear not Moses and the prophets, neither will they believe, if one rise again from the dead.

I'm pretty sure you get the point…

If you have a job, and can afford a SmartPhone you steward more than even the richest king could have dreamt to have at the time Jesus told these parables.

And no matter how poor you might actually be now, there will come a time when you have the possibility of possessing what you never could have dreamed to possess in THIS Life, on THIS Earth.

So, we are ALL in the same position, especially if we consider the state of our finances in the face of the INFINITE RICHES OF ELOHIM, rather than in the infinitely puny hill any particular Neighbor has accumulated in relationship to our own…

If we use the stuff we have been charged with stewarding to make peace with our neighbors, even with those who we would consider to be *THE LEAST* of our neighbors, now, we will possess what we never could have bought in the here-and-now, in the always now of… **FOREVER!**

And, if we don't take this action now, while we have the chance to make the choice, we won't even be able to borrow a drop of water in never-ever of Hell.

So…

GO ALL IN NOW!

BE-A-PEACEMAKER.COM

And possess what you never, ever could buy, even if you wold somehow have the Grace to find yourself to be the richest person here on Earth…

Be a Shrewd Steward, and POSSESS…
**FOREVER!**

## The Call of The Peacemaker

*FOREVER!* BE-A-PEACEMAKER.COM

Dare to Care!
Be Worthy!
Be Called "A Child of God"
**FOREVER!**

BE-A-PEACEMAKER.COM

Being a PEACEMAKER is not hard at all!
All it takes is faith, and trust…
And Just a Little MERCY-Dust.

BE-A-PEACEMAKER.COM

Be the Infinity of Happiness
You were always meant to be…

BE-A-PEACEMAKER.COM

BE-A-PEACEMAKER.COM

## The Creed of The Peacemaker – Transilluminated

Πιστεύω εἰς θεὸν πατέρα, παντοκράτορα, ποιητὴν οὐρανοῦ καὶ γῆς.
*I believe [by His Holy Grace, The Eternally Creative Golden Promise of The Eternal Community of The Ineffably Pure Light of Goodness & The Beautifully Pure Love of True Mercy, and] in God the Father, The Holy Author of The Poetic Sky of Heaven, and of Our Mother Earth,*

Καὶ (εἰς) Ἰησοῦν Χριστόν, υἱὸν αὐτοῦ τὸν μονογενῆ, τὸν κύριον ἡμῶν, ~VICTORY!~
*And (I believe [by His Holy Grace, The Eternally Creative Golden Promise of The Eternal Community of The Ineffably Pure Light of Goodness & The Beautifully Pure Love of True Mercy, and] in) Jesus the Messiah, [The Promised Seed of Sacrifice offered up to us, and planted within us by His Holy Grace, The Eternally Creative Golden Promise of The Eternal Community of The Ineffably Pure Light of Goodness & The Beautifully Pure Love of True Mercy, and] The Only Son of Our One Father, Our Lord,*

τὸν συλληφθέντα ἐκ πνεύματος ἁγίου, γεννηθέντα ἐκ Μαρίας τῆς παρθένου,
*[I believe in Jesus,] who was made to dwell among us [by His Holy Grace, The Eternally Creative Golden Promise of The Eternal Community of The Ineffably Pure Light of Goodness & The Beautifully Pure Love of True Mercy, and] of The Spirit of The Holy One; who was made to be born of Mary The Virgin [Who is She, The Promised Conqueror & Crusher of the Head of Satan, our serpentine accuser, who is she, by virtue of her unique preparation to make her especially ready for the Fullness of Time by His Holy Grace, The Eternally Creative Golden Promise of The Eternal Community of The Ineffably Pure Light of Goodness & The Beautifully Pure Love of True Mercy, and The Spirit of The Holy One, and who is she who was born of The One, True Immaculate Conception, as Queen of Heaven, and Earth, Mother of Mercy, and Queen of Grace, with whom Our Lord dwells even now, who is she who, herself by His Holy Grace, was born as the pinnacle of womanhood according to the deprecated Archetype of Athena, and is even more blessed, even being the most Blessed Among all Women, and who, herself by His Holy Grace, is the embodiment of the Magnificat, who, herself by His Holy Grace, bears the Sandals of Good News on her Feet, The Ancient Wisdom of True Light & True Love in her heart, the ancient head of The Defeated Accusing Serpent on her Mighty Shield, The Staff of The Mediatrix of All Graces, himself, in her left hand of Everlasting Mercy, and The Agility of Grace, The Holy Spirit of Victory, himself, in her right hand of Eternal Comfort];*

παθόντα ἐπὶ Ποντίου Πιλάτου, σταυρωθέντα, θανόντα, καὶ ταφέντα
*[I believe in Jesus,] who was made to suffer [by His Holy Grace, The Eternally Creative Golden Promise of The Eternal Community of The Ineffably Pure Light of Goodness & The Beautifully Pure Love of True Mercy, and] because of the action of Pontius Pilate, was made to be crucified, was made dead, and was entombed;*

κατελθόντα εἰς τὰ κατώτατα, τῇ τρίτῃ ἡμέρᾳ ἀναστάντα ἀπὸ τῶν νεκρῶν,
*[I believe in Jesus,] who was made to pass through The Netherworld [by His Holy Grace, The Eternally Creative Golden Promise of The Eternal Community of The Ineffably Pure Light of*

*Goodness & The Beautifully Pure Love of True Mercy, and], on the Third Day, was made to be raised from the dead;*

ἀνελθόντα εἰς τοὺς οὐρανούς, καθεζόμενον ἐν δεξιᾷ θεοῦ πατρὸς παντοδυνάμου,
*[I believe in Jesus,] who was made to flower back into Heaven [by His Holy Grace, The Eternally Creative Golden Promise of The Eternal Community of The Ineffably Pure Light of Goodness & The Beautifully Pure Love of True Mercy, and], has seated himself at the right hand of God, The Father, The Almighty;*

ἐκεῖθεν ἐρχόμενον κρῖναι ζῶντας καὶ νεκρούς.
*From there, [by His Holy Grace, The Eternally Creative Golden Promise of The Eternal Community of The Ineffably Pure Light of Goodness & The Beautifully Pure Love of True Mercy, and at His Holy Fiat,] he, himself, shall deign to come back to us to determine The Ultimate Destiny of both Those Who Are Alive, and Those Who Are Dead [at the time of his returning].*

Πιστεύω εἰς τὸ πνεῦμα τὸ ἅγιον, ἁγίαν καθολικὴν ἐκκλησίαν, ἁγίων κοινωνίαν,
*I believe [by His Holy Grace, The Eternally Creative Golden Promise of The Eternal Community of The Ineffably Pure Light of Goodness & The Beautifully Pure Love of True Mercy, and] in The Spirit of the Holy One, [Who IS] The Holy Universal Church, The Holy Communion,*

ἄφεσιν ἁμαρτιῶν, σαρκὸς ἀνάστασιν, ζωὴν αἰώνιον.
*The Remission of Sin, The Resurrection of the Flesh, [and] The Life of the Everlasting Ones.*

Ἀμήν.
Amen.

*VICTORY! FULL OF GRACE!*
*Χαῖρε κεχαριτωμένη*
— Luke 1:28 (DRA)

This is the creed in **THE ONE & ONLY ALMIGHTY *FOREVER***, by His Grace, and of The Ever-Existing, Uncreated, Holy Community of The Three Uniquely Essential, Inextricably Connected, Ineffably Lit, and Eternally Loving Persons who are comprised by **HE WHO IS *FOREVER*, AND WHO IS OUR PEACE, BECAUSE HIS MERCY ENDURES FOREVER** with no unnatural divisions, no contrived separations, and ALL of both the Ancient Understanding of Hebrew Scriptures, and the Ageless Wisdom of the First Century Church both of which exist to this day among us in the parish communities of The Catholic Faith Tradition, and, in celebration of Our Lady Kecharitomene, Our Queen Mother of The Prince of Peace. This version includes the full transillumination of the word παρθένου, "The Virgin," whose thought framing, yet incomplete icon of the echo of the Immaculate Conception was the long-standing, gilded statue signifying the providential patronage of Athena, "The Warrior Woman of Pure Wisdom," at The Parthenon, in Athens. This is the icon that is perfected in *The Magnificat* sung by Mary to Elizabeth, and in her perfect living out of her belief as an example of a life of the completely still faith, and the complete stillness of belief of BEING by DOING *As He [Jesus] Says* that made her The One who is Ever-Full-of-Grace, and Worthy of Assumption, and made to be eternally with Our Lord, and continually partaking **IN THE CELEBRATION OF THE WISDOM OF SHE WHO IS ALWAYS TO BE VENERATED BY OUR IMITATION OF HER HUMBLE FIAT OF SERVICE, THROUGH, AND WITH, AND IN THE AGILITY OF *HIS* GRACE.**

# The Creed of the Peacemaker – Standard Form

I believe in God,
the Father almighty,
Creator of heaven and earth,
and in Jesus Christ, his only Son, our Lord,
who was conceived by the Holy Spirit,
born of the Virgin Mary,
suffered under Pontius Pilate,
was crucified, died and was buried;
he descended into hell;
on the third day he rose again from the dead;
he ascended into heaven,
and is seated at the right hand of God the Father almighty;
from there he will come to judge the living and the dead.
I believe in the Holy Spirit,
the holy catholic Church,
the communion of saints,
the forgiveness of sins,
the resurrection of the body,
and life everlasting.
Amen.

# The Journey of The Peacemaker – Poems to Light the Path

## *Another Word for Sky*

A book of poems by Jay Michaelson, who shares the Spirit of **FOREVER!**
www.jaymichaelson.net/anotherwordforsky/

## *Psalm 23* – A Poem of David, A Peacemaker

This IS the expression of *The Creed of the Peacemaker*, which IS *The Apostles' Creed* reprocessed through the mind of the First Century Believers in Jesus who would have been living in Palestine, and IS the view of *The Creed of the Peacemaker* from the inside out, as found in Psalm 23, which ends:

- *Surely* **GOODNESS and MERCY** *shall follow me all the days of my life: and I will dwell in the house of the Lord [The Poetic Sky of Heaven],* **FOREVER**.
    **Psalm 23:6 (KJV)**

## A Trilogy of Poems by A Journeyman Peacemaker

In these works for *ageless children*, I have tried my best to explain how **YOU TOO CAN** integrate The Agility of Grace into the Reality of Your Belief in **FOREVER**, and, in the bargain, **Help Mercy Abound To Make The World a Better, Brighter Place FOR US All To Live In, and TO LOVE IN**, as you turn Your Walls into Our Shared Rainbow Bridges to The Future of Our Ultimate Happiness:

***The Little Mustard Seed Starter Pack Trilogy***
by
Grant William Shull

Which *Kindle Unlimited* Subscribers **READ For FREE**,
**AND**
Which is available at:

**LMSSPT.com**

LIVE
THE AGILITY
OF GRACE

## The Prayer of The Peacemaker

### *FOREVER*

O Elohim YHWH Adoni,
Our Melek Ha'olam,
Our Yeshua,
Our Santa Gratia —

Our One,
Holy,
Universal &
Triune God
Of The Eternal Community
Of Love —

We Beseech You —

By Your Holy Grace,
The Holy Spirit
Of Our Holy Father &
With The Holy Faith
Of Our Coadjutant Remembering
Of Our Shared Sacred Scion,
Who is The Cross-Product
Of Our Cooperation
With Your Will,
Your Mercy —

Our JESUS —

The Promised Sacrifice,
The Messiah,
The Christ,
Our King
Of Mercy —

Born
Of Your Bountiful Holy Grace &
Continually offered back
To You
In the Cloud
Of Our Witness
Of Your Holy Spirit —

Through The Work
Of Our Hands
Of Mercy —

As Our Eternal Great Hallel —

Even
Through The Sorrow
Of Our Tears —

As we sing
The Eternally Glimmering Song
Of Our Hope &
As we dance the Eternally Healing Dance
Of Our Charity —

Born
Of Your Eternally Creative Golden Promise
Of The Eternal Community
Of The Ineffably Pure Light
Of Absolute Goodness &
Of The Beautifully Pure Love
Of True Mercy —

Mediate Your Grace
To us,
We Pray,
Through Our Whole-Hearted Participation
In Your Mission
Given to Our Mother
Of Wisdom,
The Church —

With Mary,
The Assumed Virgin Mother
Of Eden's Promised Seed
Of The Creative Golden Promise
Of Your Holy Grace —

As The Queen
Of The Universe —

As The Mother
Of Mercy —

As Our Queen
of Grace —

Leading us,
As One,
To Your Communal Heart
Of Everlasting Love —

To live forever
In Perfect Peace
At The Never-Ending Point
Of Ultimate Ecstasy —

Where we shall party as ONE
For Mercy's Sake,
Always like never before —

As You engage us
With Your Ineffable Purpose,
Always for Our Own Goodwill —

Always with The Agility of Grace —

As You engage us
In The Ultimate &
Never-Ending Act
Of The Infinite Happiness
Of Divine Intercourse
With You &
With Our Likewise Merciful Neighbors —

Where Time Shall Tick &
Tear Shall Drop No More —

For Your Mercy ENDURES...

**FOREVER!**

AMEN.

## The Meditation of The Peacemaker

**FOREVER** is, indeed, the name of God (Elohim YHWH Adoni), because **FOREVER** is his very nature, and the substance, and the realization by His Holy Grace, The Eternally Creative Golden Promise of The Eternal Community of The Ineffably Pure Light of Goodness & The Beautifully Pure Love of True Mercy, His Unconditionally True Love, and so the practice of the **FOREVER** Love of Mercy stands in contrast to the popular practice of "Unconditional Love" which  claims to make no judgements, but is, in reality a narcissistic, hubristic, hyperbole of half-truth born of the same vain bite of The Fruit of Eden that doomed ALL OF US unto what God has turned into the Blessed Fault of Adam & Eve, just as he did the pit of Joseph's Bloody Coat.

This is why Jesus did not ask us to either believe unconditionally, nor to love unconditionally, but called us, instead, to believe in The **FOREVER TRUTH** (and by logical extension discard transient, mortally fatal lies), so that we might also worship in Spirit, and in Truth, with the ever-creative work of our hands of Mercy according to the what he gave us as the "Golden Commandments" in the Gospels, particularly in Mark, as he delineated the nature of **FOREVER** to a student of the Law, as he said:

- *The first commandment of all is, Hear, O Israel: the Lord thy God is one God. And thou shalt love the Lord thy God, with thy whole heart, and with thy whole soul, and with thy whole mind, and with thy whole strength. This is the first commandment. And the second is like to it: Thou shalt love thy neighbour as thyself. There is no other commandment greater than these.*

    **Mark 12:29-31 (DRA)**

**So...**

What happens when **Belief is not something you have, but why you are?** What happens when you **no longer think of yourself as possessing belief, but of belief possessing you in your stillness, even as you act decisively for the good** of others on the truth of that belief?

What happens when Truth, and Beauty, and Goodness are not what you seek to posses, or what you strive to produce, but are simply what follow you home, so that you may offer them up as an infinite, and ever-ready supply of Happiness to your Neighbors? What happens when you no longer "make" contributions, but allow your contribution to make you?

What happens when Faith, Hope, and Charity no longer are what you do, but who you are? What happens when you become BELIEF IN HIMSELF WHO IS **FOREVER**? Then, the doing of belief IS being, because Elohim IS The Eternal Community of The Agility of Grace, of The Creative Golden Promise of Love, who's very nature is YHWH (both TO BE **FOREVER** & TO DO **FOREVER**)

**Therefore non-belief, and by extension, non-doing is death.**

So let us all pray along with the man who sought Jesus out to remove the unclean spirit from his son:

- *I do believe, Lord: help my unbelief.*
    **Mark 9:23 (DRA)**

Because as Jesus advised, before he undertook the performance of this great work of Mercy for this man:

- *If thou canst believe, all things are possible to him that believeth.*
    **Mark 9:22 (DRA)**

**INDEED, ALL THINGS are possible to him that believes**, because:

- *Our Final Purpose IS To Believe.*

- *Our Formal Purpose IS To Demonstrate Our Belief with WHAT WE DO!*

- *And our Telos **IS TO BE AT** Peace with Our Belief in Him who is the Promise of that Belief [which is to be Ecstatically **AT** One with Him in our Creative Dance of **FOREVER** who is The Eternally Creative Golden Promise of The Eternal Community of The Ineffably Pure Light of Goodness & The Beautifully Pure Love of True Mercy, and therefore, **TO BECOME EXISTENCE**, Himself as MERCY WHO ENDURES **FOREVER**!].*

**BECAUSE PURE EXISTENCE KNOWS NO BOUNDS, JUST AS PURE MERCY KNOWS NO BOUNDS!**

**BECAUSE ONLY PURE TRUTH CAN BE BELIEVED IN... PURELY, AND COMPLETELY... HE WHO IS THE PURE TRUTH OF EXISTENCE, AND THE MERCY WHO ENDURES FOREVER IS THE ONLY FORCE OF BEING** in both this Universe, and whatever lies ahead, **IS THE HE WHO CAN LITERALLY EMPOWER US TO ACCOMPLISH, THAT IS TO <u>DO</u>: ALL THINGS!**

- *This is why we suffer unashamedly with St. Paul to encourage the **Total Belief in Mercy**, whom, as **Psalm 136 [Psalm 135 (DRA)**, The Great Hallel tells us, "Endureth **FOREVER**,"* *whom he had come to know through the Ministry of Onesiphorus, who visited him in prison (Corporal Act of Mercy — CAM #6) as he writes in his second letter to Timothy.*

This is why St. Paul puts such a fine point on the "Unabashed Willingness to Suffer for The PROMISE of God", which, apparently, was part of what he had seen in that flash of Holy Glory that blinded him to nothing but the PURE TRUTH OF EXISTENCE on fated path to Damascus:

- *Be not thou therefore ashamed of the testimony of our Lord, nor of me his prisoner: but labour with the gospel, according to the power of God, Who hath delivered us and called us by his holy calling, not according to our works, but according to his own purpose and grace, which was given us in Christ Jesus before the times of the world. But is now made manifest by the illumination of our Saviour Jesus Christ, who hath destroyed death, and hath brought to light life and incorruption by the gospel: Wherein I am appointed a preacher, and an apostle, and teacher of the Gentiles. For which cause I also suffer these things: but I am not ashamed. **For I know whom I have believed, and I am certain that he is able to keep that which I have committed unto him, against that day.***

    **2 Tim 1:8-12 (DRA)**

And sin [such as eating of The Fruit of The Tree of The Knowledge of Good & Evil] is to behave in ways that <u>demonstrate</u> our non-belief.

In a pure, and perfect world we would need only to demonstrate our belief by behaving (TO BE through our acts of being) as we were instructed by The Promise of Belief himself, and avoiding the one thing (the way of being not) that we were instructed to avoid (unbelief in His Holy Grace, The Eternally Creative Golden Promise of The Eternal Community of The Ineffably Pure Light of Goodness & The Beautifully Pure Love of True Mercy, and, by extension, his Perfect Provision for Our Eternal Life, and) thus simply BE.

In the fallen world, we who would follow The Way of Mercy as The Way of Being that Leads to Pure Belief must, as St. Paul writes to the Ephesians in Chapter 4, sustainably avoid the ways of being that demonstrates our non-belief, continually be renewed in our mind by His Holy Grace, The Eternally Creative Golden Promise of The Eternal Community of The Ineffably Pure Light of Goodness & The Beautifully Pure Love of True Mercy, and, be recreated by recreating the World around us with the way of being that makes both us, and Our Neighbors, ready to believe anew, and then following this way of being, which is The Way of Mercy, to demonstrate, once again as the newly *Quasi Modo,* yet still fully made Makers of Peace, and, as such, The Children of God. Ready to believe our belief by <u>DOING THE TRUTH IN CHARITY</u>, which is the way of doing the work of our hands for Mercy's Sake as we were originally charged when the world was still perfect, until we do FULLY KNOW [aka Have Divine Intercourse with] GOD, again, and, in a like manner, know our Neighbors [cf. the Gethemane Prayer] as ourselves who party with us as "members one of another" for Mercy's Sake each, and every day, even until the hour of our death, even until we all meet as ONE beyond time itself, when hours of petty pacing time, and the tears of vapid biting sorrow are no more; where we are finally, and uncontrovertibly delivered INTO **FOREVER** AS The Unity of the Infinities of Happiness we were always meant to be:

- *Until we all meet into the unity of faith, and of the knowledge of the Son of God, unto a perfect man, unto the measure of the age of the fulness of Christ; That henceforth we be no more children tossed to and fro, and carried about with every wind of doctrine by the wickedness of men, by cunning craftiness, by which they lie in wait to deceive. But doing the truth in charity, we may in all things grow up in him who is the head, even Christ: From whom the whole body, being compacted and fitly joined together, by what every joint supplieth, according to the operation in the measure of every part, maketh increase of the body, unto the edifying of itself in charity. This then I say and testify in the Lord: That henceforward you walk not as also the Gentiles walk in the vanity of their mind, Having their understanding darkened, being alienated from the life of God through the ignorance that is in them, because of the blindness of their hearts. Who despairing, have given themselves up to lasciviousness, unto the working of all uncleanness, unto the working of all uncleanness, unto covetousness. But you have not so learned Christ; If so be that you have heard him, and have been taught in him, as the truth is in Jesus: To put off, according to former conversation, the old man, who is corrupted according to the desire of error. And be renewed in the spirit of your mind: And put on the new man, who according to God is created in justice and holiness of truth. Wherefore putting away lying, speak ye the truth every man with his neighbour; for we are members one of another.*

    **Ephesians 4:13-25 (DRA)**

Therefore, until we are finally, and for all of Eternity "made one", let us PRACTICE our *quasi modo* selves INTO WORKS OF MERCY which we deliver at the doorstep of our Neighbors.

Let this be the hope of our faith, the demonstrated delivery of our belief, not simply as what we are called to DO, but as who we ARE (clay pots full of divine kindness), even as if we have already been fully made to **ENDURE *FOREVER*,** even so that we might **BE *FOREVER*.**

# The Profession of the Peacemaker

## The Dignity of *Tikkun Olam*

Mark 6:37

- *And the Lord God made for Adam and his wife, garments of skins, and clothed them.*
  <u>Genesis 3:21 (DRA)</u>

## The Mercy of Abram to Preserve The Dignity of Sodom

**13:13** Now the people of Sodom were wicked and were sinning greatly against the Lord.

**14** The Lord said to Abram after Lot had parted from him, "Look around from where you are, to the north and south, to the east and west. **15** All the land that you see I will give to you and your offspring[a] forever. **16** I will make your offspring like the dust of the earth, so that if anyone could count the dust, then your offspring could be counted. **17** Go, walk through the length and breadth of the land, for I am giving it to you."

**18** So Abram went to live near the great trees of Mamre at Hebron, where he pitched his tents. There he built an altar to the Lord.

**14:1** At the time when Amraphel was king of Shinar,[b] Arioch king of Ellasar, Kedorlaomer king of Elam and Tidal king of Goyim, **2** these kings went to war against Bera king of Sodom, Birsha king of Gomorrah, Shinab king of Admah, Shemeber king of Zeboyim, and the king of Bela (that is, Zoar). **3** All these latter kings joined forces in the Valley of Siddim (that is, the Dead Sea Valley). **4** For twelve years they had been subject to Kedorlaomer, but in the thirteenth year they rebelled.

**5** In the fourteenth year, Kedorlaomer and the kings allied with him went out and defeated the Rephaites in Ashteroth Karnaim, the Zuzites in Ham, the Emites in Shaveh Kiriathaim **6** and the Horites in the hill country of Seir, as far as El Paran near the desert. **7** Then they turned back and went to En Mishpat (that is, Kadesh), and they conquered the whole territory of the Amalekites, as well as the Amorites who were living in Hazezon Tamar.

**8** Then the king of Sodom, the king of Gomorrah, the king of Admah, the king of Zeboyim and the king of Bela (that is, Zoar) marched out and drew up their battle lines in the Valley of Siddim **9** against Kedorlaomer king of Elam, Tidal king of Goyim, Amraphel king of Shinar and Arioch king of Ellasar—four kings against five. **10** Now the Valley of Siddim was full of tar pits, and when the kings of Sodom and Gomorrah fled, some of the men fell into them and the rest fled to the hills. **11** The four kings seized all the goods of Sodom and Gomorrah and all their food; then they went away. **12** They also carried off Abram's nephew Lot and his possessions, since he was living in Sodom.

**13** A man who had escaped came and reported this to Abram the Hebrew. Now Abram was living near the great trees of Mamre the Amorite, a brother[c] of Eshkol and Aner, all of whom were allied with Abram. **14** When Abram heard that his relative had been taken captive, he called out the 318 trained men born in his household and went in pursuit as far as Dan.

**15** During the night Abram divided his men to attack them and he routed them, pursuing them as far as Hobah, north of Damascus. **16** He recovered all the goods and brought back his relative Lot and his possessions, together with the women and the other people.

**17** After Abram returned from defeating Kedorlaomer and the kings allied with him, the king of Sodom came out to meet him in the Valley of Shaveh (that is, the King's Valley).

**18** Then Melchizedek king of Salem brought out bread and wine. He was priest of God Most High, **19** and he blessed Abram, saying,

"Blessed be Abram by God Most High,

Creator of heaven and earth.

**20**

And praise be to God Most High,

who delivered your enemies into your hand."

Then Abram gave him a tenth of everything.

**21** The king of Sodom said to Abram, "Give me the people and keep the goods for yourself."

**22** But Abram said to the king of Sodom, "With raised hand I have sworn an oath to the Lord, God Most High, Creator of heaven and earth, **23** that I will accept nothing belonging to you, not even a thread or the strap of a sandal, so that you will never be able to say, 'I made Abram rich.' **24** I will accept nothing but what my men have eaten and the share that belongs to the men who went with me—to Aner, Eshkol and Mamre. Let them have their share."

**15:1** After this, the word of the Lord came to Abram in a vision:

"Do not be afraid, Abram.

I am your shield,

your very great reward."

**2** But Abram said, "Sovereign Lord, what can you give me since I remain childless and the one who will inherit[f] my estate is Eliezer of Damascus?" **3** And Abram said, "You have given me no children; so a servant in my household will be my heir."

**4** Then the word of the Lord came to him: "This man will not be your heir, but a son who is your own flesh and blood will be your heir." **5** He took him outside and said, "Look up at the sky and count the stars—if indeed you can count them." Then he said to him, "So shall your offspring[g] be."

**6** Abram believed the Lord, and he credited it to him as righteousness.

Genesis 13:13-15:6 (DRA)

# The Sermon for The Peacemaker

## Matthew Chapters 5-7 (DRA)

**5:1** And seeing the multitudes, he went up into a mountain, and when he was set down, his disciples came unto him.

**2** And opening his mouth, he taught them, saying:

**3** Blessed are the poor in spirit: for theirs is the kingdom of heaven.

**4** Blessed are the meek: for they shall possess the land.

**5** Blessed are they that mourn: for they shall be comforted.

**6** Blessed are they that hunger and thirst after justice: for they shall have their fill.

**7** Blessed are the merciful: for they shall obtain mercy.

**8** Blessed are the clean of heart: for they shall see God.

**9** Blessed are the peacemakers: for they shall be called children of God.

**10** Blessed are they that suffer persecution for justice' sake: for theirs is the kingdom of heaven.

**11** Blessed are ye when they shall revile you, and persecute you, and speak all that is evil against you, untruly, for my sake:

**12** Be glad and rejoice, for your reward is very great in heaven. For so they persecuted the prophets that were before you.

**13** You are the salt of the earth. But if the salt lose its savour, wherewith shall it be salted? It is good for nothing any more but to be cast out, and to be trodden on by men.

**14** You are the light of the world. A city seated on a mountain cannot be hid.

**15** Neither do men light a candle and put it under a bushel, but upon a candlestick, that it may shine to all that are in the house.

**16** So let your light shine before men, that they may see your good works, and glorify your Father who is in heaven.

**17** Do not think that I am come to destroy the law, or the prophets. I am not come to destroy, but to fulfill.

**18** For amen I say unto you, till heaven and earth pass, one jot, or one tittle shall not pass of the law, till all be fulfilled.

**19** He therefore that shall break one of these least commandments, and shall so teach men, shall be called the least in the kingdom of heaven. But he that shall do and teach, he shall be called great in the kingdom of heaven.

**20** For I tell you, that unless your justice abound more than that of the scribes and Pharisees, you shall not enter into the kingdom of heaven.

**21** You have heard that it was said to them of old: Thou shalt not kill. And whosoever shall kill shall be in danger of the judgment.

**22** But I say to you, that whosoever is angry with his brother, shall be in danger of the judgment. And whosoever shall say to his brother, Raca, shall be in danger of the council. And whosoever shall say, Thou Fool, shall be in danger of hell fire.

**23** If therefore thou offer thy gift at the altar, and there thou remember that thy brother hath any thing against thee;

**24** Leave there thy offering before the altar, and go first to be reconciled to thy brother: and then coming thou shalt offer thy gift.

**25** Be at agreement with thy adversary betimes, whilst thou art in the way with him: lest perhaps the adversary deliver thee to the judge, and the judge deliver thee to the officer, and thou be cast into prison.

**26** Amen I say to thee, thou shalt not go out from thence till thou repay the last farthing.

**27** You have heard that it was said to them of old: Thou shalt not commit adultery.

**28** But I say to you, that whosoever shall look on a woman to lust after her, hath already committed adultery with her in his heart.

**29** And if thy right eye scandalize thee, pluck it out and cast it from thee. For it is expedient for thee that one of thy members should perish, rather than that thy whole body be cast into hell.

**30** And if thy right hand scandalize thee, cut it off, and cast it from thee: for it is expedient for thee that one of thy members should perish, rather than that thy whole body be cast into hell.

**31** And it hath been said, Whosoever shall put away his wife, let him give her a bill of divorce.

**32** But I say to you, that whosoever shall put away his wife, excepting for the cause of fornication, maketh her to commit adultery: and he that shall marry her that is put away, committeth adultery.

**33** Again you have heard that it was said to them of old, Thou shalt not forswear thyself: but thou shalt perform thy oaths to the Lord.

**34** But I say to you not to swear at all, neither by heaven, for it is the throne of God:

**35** Nor by the earth, for it is his footstool: nor by Jerusalem, for it is the city of the great king:

**36** Neither shalt thou swear by thy head, because thou canst not make one hair white or black.

**37** But let your speech be yea, yea: no, no: and that which is over and above these, is of evil.

**38** You have heard that it hath been said, An eye for an eye, and a tooth for a tooth.

**39** But I say to you not to resist evil: but if one strike thee on thy right cheek, turn to him also the other:

**40** And if a man will contend with thee in judgment, and take away thy coat, let go thy cloak also unto him.

**41** And whosoever will force thee one mile, go with him other two,

**42** Give to him that asketh of thee and from him that would borrow of thee turn not away.

**43** You have heard that it hath been said, Thou shalt love thy neighbour, and hate thy enemy.

**44** But I say to you, Love your enemies: do good to them that hate you: and pray for them that persecute and calumniate you:

**45** That you may be the children of your Father who is in heaven, who maketh his sun to rise upon the good, and bad, and raineth upon the just and the unjust.

**46** For if you love them that love you, what reward shall you have? do not even the publicans this?

**47** And if you salute your brethren only, what do you more? do not also the heathens this?

**48** Be you therefore perfect, as also your heavenly Father is perfect.

**6:1** Take heed that you do not your justice before men, to be seen by them: otherwise you shall not have a reward of your Father who is in heaven.

**2** Therefore when thou dost an almsdeed, sound not a trumpet before thee, as the hypocrites do in the synagogues and in the streets, that they may be honoured by men. Amen I say to you, they have received their reward.

**3** But when thou dost alms, let not thy left hand know what thy right hand doth.

**4** That thy alms may be in secret, and thy Father who seeth in secret will repay thee.

**5** And when ye pray, you shall not be as the hypocrites, that love to stand and pray in the synagogues and corners of the streets, that they may be seen by men: Amen I say to you, they have received their reward.

**6** But thou when thou shalt pray, enter into thy chamber, and having shut the door, pray to thy Father in secret: and thy Father who seeth in secret will repay thee.

**7** And when you are praying, speak not much, as the heathens. For they think that in their much speaking they may be heard.

**8** Be not you therefore like to them, for your Father knoweth what is needful for you, before you ask him.

**9** Thus therefore shall you pray: Our Father who art in heaven, hallowed be thy name.

**10** Thy kingdom come. Thy will be done on earth as it is in heaven.

**11** Give us this day our supersubstantial bread.

**12** And forgive us our debts, as we also forgive our debtors.

**13** And lead us not into temptation. But deliver us from evil. Amen.

**14** For if you will forgive men their offences, your heavenly Father will forgive you also your offences.

**15** But if you will not forgive men, neither will your Father forgive you your offences.

**16** And when you fast, be not as the hypocrites, sad. For they disfigure their faces, that they may appear unto men to fast. Amen I say to you, they have received their reward.

**17** But thou, when thou fastest anoint thy head, and wash thy face;

**18** That thou appear not to men to fast, but to thy Father who is in secret: and thy Father who seeth in secret, will repay thee.

**19** Lay not up to yourselves treasures on earth: where the rust, and moth consume, and where thieves break through and steal.

**20** But lay up to yourselves treasures in heaven: where neither the rust nor moth doth consume, and where thieves do not break through, nor steal.

**21** For where thy treasure is, there is thy heart also.

**22** The light of thy body is thy eye. If thy eye be single, thy whole body shall be lightsome.

**23** But if thy eye be evil thy whole body shall be darksome. If then the light that is in thee, be darkness: the darkness itself how great shall it be!

**24** No man can serve two masters. For either he will hate the one, and love the other: or he will sustain the one, and despise the other. You cannot serve God and mammon.

**25** Therefore I say to you, be not solicitous for your life, what you shall eat, nor for your body, what you shall put on. Is not the life more than the meat: and the body more than the raiment?

**26** Behold the birds of the air, for they neither sow, nor do they reap, nor gather into barns: and your heavenly Father feedeth them. Are not you of much more value than they?

**27** And which of you by taking thought, can add to his stature by one cubit?

**28** And for raiment why are you solicitous? Consider the lilies of the field, how they grow: they labour not, neither do they spin.

**29** But I say to you, that not even Solomon in all his glory was arrayed as one of these.

**30** And if the grass of the field, which is to day, and to morrow is cast into the oven, God doth so clothe: how much more you, O ye of little faith?

**31** Be not solicitous therefore, saying, What shall we eat: or what shall we drink, or wherewith shall we be clothed?

**32** For after all these things do the heathens seek. For your Father knoweth that you have need of all these things.

**33** Seek ye therefore first the kingdom of God, and his justice, and all these things shall be added unto you.

**34** Be not therefore solicitous for to morrow; for the morrow will be solicitous for itself. Sufficient for the day is the evil thereof.

**7:1** Judge not, that you may not be judged,

**2** For with what judgment you judge, you shall be judged: and with what measure you mete, it shall be measured to you again.

**3** And why seest thou the mote that is in thy brother's eye; and seest not the beam that is in thy own eye?

**4** Or how sayest thou to thy brother: Let me cast the mote out of thy eye; and behold a beam is in thy own eye?

**5** Thou hypocrite, cast out first the beam in thy own eye, and then shalt thou see to cast out the mote out of thy brother's eye.

**6** Give not that which is holy to dogs; neither cast ye your pearls before swine, lest perhaps they trample them under their feet, and turning upon you, they tear you.

**7** Ask, and it shall be given you: seek, and you shall find: knock, and it shall be opened to you.

**8** For every one that asketh, receiveth: and he that seeketh, findeth: and to him that knocketh, it shall be opened.

**9** Or what man is there among you, of whom if his son shall ask bread, will he reach him a stone?

**10** Or if he shall ask him a fish, will he reach him a serpent?

**11** If you then being evil, know how to give good gifts to your children: how much more will your Father who is in heaven, give good things to them that ask him?

**12** All things therefore whatsoever you would that men should do to you, do you also to them. For this is the law and the prophets.

**13** Enter ye in at the narrow gate: for wide is the gate, and broad is the way that leadeth to destruction, and many there are who go in thereat.

**14** How narrow is the gate, and strait is the way that leadeth to life: and few there are that find it!

**15** Beware of false prophets, who come to you in the clothing of sheep, but inwardly they are ravening wolves.

**16** By their fruits you shall know them. Do men gather grapes of thorns, or figs of thistles?

**17** Even so every good tree bringeth forth good fruit, and the evil tree bringeth forth evil fruit.

**18** A good tree cannot bring forth evil fruit, neither can an evil tree bring forth good fruit.

**19** Every tree that bringeth not forth good fruit, shall be cut down, and shall be cast into the fire.

**20** Wherefore by their fruits you shall know them.

**21** Not every one that saith to me, Lord, Lord, shall enter into the kingdom of heaven: but he that doth the will of my Father who is in heaven, he shall enter into the kingdom of heaven.

**22** Many will say to me in that day: Lord, Lord, have not we prophesied in thy name, and cast out devils in thy name, and done many miracles in thy name?

**23** And then will I profess unto them, I never knew you: depart from me, you that work iniquity.

**24** Every one therefore that heareth these my words, and doth them, shall be likened to a wise man that built his house upon a rock,

**25** And the rain fell, and the floods came, and the winds blew, and they beat upon that house, and it fell not, for it was founded on a rock.

**26** And every one that heareth these my words, and doth them not, shall be like a foolish man that built his house upon the sand,

**27** And the rain fell, and the floods came, and the winds blew, and they beat upon that house, and it fell, and great was the fall thereof.

**28** And it came to pass when Jesus had fully ended these words, the people were in admiration at his doctrine.

**29** For he was teaching them as one having power, and not as the scribes and Pharisees.

# The Judgement of The Peacemaker

## Be a Sheep: Matthew Chapters 24-25 (DRA)

**24:1** And Jesus being come out of the temple, went away. And his disciples came to shew him the buildings of the temple.

**2** And he answering, said to them: Do you see all these things? Amen I say to you there shall not be left here a stone upon a stone that shall not be destroyed.

**3** And when he was sitting on mount Olivet, the disciples came to him privately, saying: Tell us when shall these things be? and what shall be the sign of thy coming, and of the consummation of the world?

**4** And Jesus answering, said to them: Take heed that no man seduce you:

**5** For many will come in my name saying, I am Christ: and they will seduce many.

**6** And you shall hear of wars and rumours of wars. See that ye be not troubled. For these things must come to pass, but the end is not yet.

**7** For nation shall rise against nation, and kingdom against kingdom; and there shall be pestilences, and famines, and earthquakes in places:

**8** Now all these are the beginnings of sorrows.

**9** Then shall they deliver you up to be afflicted, and shall put you to death: and you shall be hated by all nations for my name's sake.

**10** And then shall many be scandalized: and shall betray one another: and shall hate one another.

**11** And many false prophets shall rise, and shall seduce many.

**12** And because iniquity hath abounded, the charity of many shall grow cold.

**13** But he that shall persevere to the end, he shall be saved.

**14** And this gospel of the kingdom, shall be preached in the whole world, for a testimony to all nations, and then shall the consummation come.

**15** When therefore you shall see the abomination of desolation, which was spoken of by Daniel the prophet, standing in the holy place: he that readeth let him understand.

**16** Then they that are in Judea, let them flee to the mountains:

**17** And he that is on the housetop, let him not come down to take any thing out of his house:

**18** And he that is in the field, let him not go back to take his coat.

**19** And woe to them that are with child, and that give suck in those days.

**20** But pray that your flight be not in the winter, or on the sabbath.

**21** For there shall be then great tribulation, such as hath not been from the beginning of the world until now, neither shall be.

**22** And unless those days had been shortened, no flesh should be saved: but for the sake of the elect those days shall be shortened.

**23** Then if any man shall say to you: Lo here is Christ, or there, do not believe him.

**24** For there shall arise false Christs and false prophets, and shall shew great signs and wonders, insomuch as to deceive (if possible) even the elect.

**25** Behold I have told it to you, beforehand.

**26** If therefore they shall say to you: Behold he is in the desert, go ye not out: Behold he is in the closets, believe it not.

**27** For as lightning cometh out of the east, and appeareth even into the west: so shall the coming of the Son of man be.

**28** Wheresoever the body shall be, there shall the eagles also be gathered together.

**29** And immediately after the tribulation of those days, the sun shall be darkened and the moon shall not give her light, and the stars shall fall from heaven, and the powers of heaven shall be moved:

**30** And then shall appear the sign of the Son of man in heaven: and then shall all tribes of the earth mourn: and they shall see the Son of man coming in the clouds of heaven with much power and majesty.

**31** And he shall send his angels with a trumpet, and a great voice: and they shall gather together his elect from the four winds, from the farthest parts of the heavens to the utmost bounds of them.

**32** And from the fig tree learn a parable: When the branch thereof is now tender, and the leaves come forth, you know that summer is nigh.

**33** So you also, when you shall see all these things, know ye that it is nigh, even at the doors.

**34** Amen I say to you, that this generation shall not pass, till all these things be done.

**35** Heaven and earth shall pass, but my words shall not pass.

**36** But of that day and hour no one knoweth, not the angels of heaven, but the Father alone.

**37** And as in the days of Noe, so shall also the coming of the Son of man be.

**38** For as in the days before the flood, they were eating and drinking, marrying and giving in marriage, even till that day in which Noe entered into the ark,

**39** And they knew not till the flood came, and took them all away; so also shall the coming of the Son of man be.

**40** Then two shall be in the field: one shall be taken, and one shall be left.

**41** Two women shall be grinding at the mill: one shall be taken, and one shall be left.

**42** Watch ye therefore, because ye know not what hour your Lord will come.

**43** But know this ye, that if the goodman of the house knew at what hour the thief would come, he would certainly watch, and would not suffer his house to be broken open.

**44** Wherefore be you also ready, because at what hour you know not the Son of man will come.

**45** Who, thinkest thou, is a faithful and wise servant, whom his lord hath appointed over his family, to give them meat in season.

**46** Blessed is that servant, whom when his lord shall come he shall find so doing.

**47** Amen I say to you, he shall place him over all his goods.

**48** But if that evil servant shall say in his heart: My lord is long a coming:

**49** And shall begin to strike his fellow servants, and shall eat and drink with drunkards:

**50** The lord of that servant shall come in a day that he hopeth not, and at an hour that he knoweth not:

**51** And shall separate him, and appoint his portion with the hypocrites. There shall be weeping and gnashing of teeth.

**25:1** Then shall the kingdom of heaven be like to ten virgins, who taking their lamps went out to meet the bridegroom and the bride.

**2** And five of them were foolish, and five wise.

**3** But the five foolish, having taken their lamps, did not take oil with them:

**4** But the wise took oil in their vessels with the lamps.

**5** And the bridegroom tarrying, they all slumbered and slept.

**6** And at midnight there was a cry made: Behold the bridegroom cometh, go ye forth to meet him.

**7** Then all those virgins arose and trimmed their lamps.

**8** And the foolish said to the wise: Give us of your oil, for our lamps are gone out.

**9** The wise answered, saying: Lest perhaps there be not enough for us and for you, go ye rather to them that sell, and buy for yourselves.

**10** Now whilst they went to buy, the bridegroom came: and they that were ready, went in with him to the marriage, and the door was shut.

**11** But at last come also the other virgins, saying: Lord, Lord, open to us.

**12** But he answering said: Amen I say to you, I know you not.

**13** Watch ye therefore, because you know not the day nor the hour.

**14** For even as a man going into a far country, called his servants, and delivered to them his goods;

**15** And to one he gave five talents, and to another two, and to another one, to every one according to his proper ability: and immediately he took his journey.

**16** And he that had received the five talents, went his way, and traded with the same, and gained other five.

**17** And in like manner he that had received the two, gained other two.

**18** But he that had received the one, going his way digged into the earth, and hid his lord's money.

**19** But after a long time the lord of those servants came, and reckoned with them.

**20** And he that had received the five talents coming, brought other five talents, saying: Lord, thou didst deliver to me five talents, behold I have gained other five over and above.

**21** His lord said to him: Well done, good and faithful servant, because thou hast been faithful over a few things, I will place thee over many things: enter thou into the joy of thy lord.

**22** And he also that had received the two talents came and said: Lord, thou deliveredst two talents to me: behold I have gained other two.

**23** His lord said to him: Well done, good and faithful servant: because thou hast been faithful over a few things, I will place thee over many things: enter thou into the joy of thy lord.

**24** But he that had received the one talent, came and said: Lord, I know that thou art a hard man; thou reapest where thou hast not sown, and gatherest where thou hast not strewed.

**25** And being afraid I went and hid thy talent in the earth: behold here thou hast that which is thine.

**26** And his lord answering, said to him: Wicked and slothful servant, thou knewest that I reap where I sow not, and gather where I have not strewed:

**27** Thou oughtest therefore to have committed my money to the bankers, and at my coming I should have received my own with usury.

**28** Take ye away therefore the talent from him, and give it to him that hath ten talents.

**29** For to every one that hath shall be given, and he shall abound: but from him that hath not, that also which he seemeth to have shall be taken away.

**30** And the unprofitable servant cast ye out into the exterior darkness. There shall be weeping and gnashing of teeth.

**31 And when the Son of man shall come in his majesty, and all the angels with him, then shall he sit upon the seat of his majesty.**

**32 And all nations shall be gathered together before him, and he shall separate them one from another, as the shepherd separateth the sheep from the goats:**

**33 And he shall set the sheep on his right hand, but the goats on his left.**

**34 Then shall the king say to them that shall be on his right hand: Come, ye blessed of my Father, possess you the kingdom prepared for you from the foundation of the world.**

**35 For I was hungry, and you gave me to eat; I was thirsty, and you gave me to drink; I was a stranger, and you took me in:**

**36 Naked, and you covered me: sick, and you visited me: I was in prison, and you came to me.**

**37 Then shall the just answer him, saying: Lord, when did we see thee hungry, and fed thee; thirsty, and gave thee drink?**

**38 And when did we see thee a stranger, and took thee in? or naked, and covered thee?**

**39 Or when did we see thee sick or in prison, and came to thee?**

**40 And the king answering, shall say to them: Amen I say to you, as long as you did it to one of these my least brethren, you did it to me.** *[Regarding the word "brethren" here — remember the words of Matthew 5:42-48 above, for Jesus is the Brother of ALL of us.]*

**41 Then he shall say to them also that shall be on his left hand: Depart from me, you cursed, into everlasting fire which was prepared for the devil and his angels.**

**42 For I was hungry, and you gave me not to eat: I was thirsty, and you gave me not to drink.**

**43 I was a stranger, and you took me not in: naked, and you covered me not: sick and in prison, and you did not visit me.**

**44 Then they also shall answer him, saying: Lord, when did we see thee hungry, or thirsty, or a stranger, or naked, or sick, or in prison, and did not minister to thee?**

**45** Then he shall answer them, saying: Amen I say to you, as long as you did it not to one of these least, neither did you do it to me. *[Notice the absence even of the word "brethren" here, emphasizing the universality of the Judgement for Mercy's Sake.]*

**46** And these *[goats on the left]* shall go into everlasting punishment: but the just *[these sheep on the right]*, into life everlasting.

# The Practice of The Peacemaker – *Dignity at Work*

## The Agility of Grace

**Turning Everything Right-Side Up Again**

Ever since the Incident at The Tree of The Knowledge of Good & Evil, the world of work has been upside-down.

The Hubris, Hyperbole, and Half-Truths used by Satan to make the largest land grab in history, and the FUDS of OPML that left Adam & Eve with the worst Real Estate deal, and the worst Buyer's Remorse Hangover Headache of all times soon turned into the first labor dispute that drew the first human blood in the first human-on-human act of murder ever.

Why?

Because Cain didn't want to do The Work of Mercy. He was lazy. He only wanted to do The Work of The Curse, the work of The Land. And since he was bigger, and older and stronger than Able, he asserted one of the worst management tropes in history as well: *Might Makes Right*.

All of this, because he saw life as a zero-sum game where there are only "winners" and "losers", and because he was not at all pleased with the hand he was dealt, because he didn't think it was "fair".

As a worker of the land, Cain did not have access to the flocks that were required to make a proper sacrifice to wipe the curse of the land off his pitiful body. So, instead of acting with the Caritas Love, and Goodwill embodied by the sacrifice itself, and helping to point the way to the Ultimate Sacrifice of Jesus, The Messiah, Mercy Himself, on the cross as did Able, who believed God at his word, and by his ACTION IN EDEN, he had heard tell of by his father, Adam, instead, followed the "Other People Must Lose so that I can win mantra", the same mantra that Jesus told us in Matthew 25 would get us the "thumbs down" of our own personal goat parade of ONE to Hell.

And then he pursued the logical extension of OPML with the FUDS of Fear, Uncertainty, Doubts, Shame, and Sorrow by:

- *Fearing that He had "lost" because God was "playing favorites".*

- *Taking Offense because he thought God was being "unfair" by accepting Ables worthy sacrifice while not accepting his own unworthy offering of "doing what he could with what he had been given" instead of "being the doer of goo" and thus repeating his parents' error of being uncertain that Elohim knew exactly what he was doing, and was truly good.*

- *Holding a Grudge, and murdering Truth, just like Pontus Pilot did several thousands of years later, because he then doubted himself, and God, and Able, and whether or not anything really mattered, or there was any Truth at all in the Bohemian Landscape that was his cursed home.*

- *Harbored that grudge until his shame turned it into the vitriol of hate that would manifest itself as the crude weapon of Sorrow he would opportunistically turn in to a projectile of death later in the day*

- *AND THEN… filled with Hubris, and the self-pity of his Hyperbolic, FUDS-filled reaction to the rejection of his scoff-law sacrifice, he followed the way of the goat by rejecting The Agility of Grace who would have otherwise guided him to the peace of collaboration with Able, so that a trade of collaborative differentials would have allowed both of their boats to rise together in a sin-flooded world.*

- *Cain then used the mechanism of the Half-Truth that broke the entire world just one generation earlier, and, perhaps screaming the equivalent of "FAKE NEWS" he treacherously took advantage of the trust of Able, and brought a rock of scorn down on his brother's head so that he, Cain, and he, Cain alone, would rule both the fields, and the flocks…ALL for him, and less than nothing at all for Able that "sad" Able, whose blood still cries out even from our dreadfully broken skirmishes for fleeting fields of meaningless corn even until this day.*

And in the aftermath, Tubal-Cain, The Scourge of Noah, upheld his kin's ideal of land, and folk, and blood, and turned Cain's Gambit into the FUDS-based pyramid management style that has persisted until this day, misleading misguided mobs of magpies to believe that the only way to get ahead is to operate from the position of OPML, "Other People Must Lose". And the bigger the loss for the "loser", the better it is for the "winner", neither of whom are befitting to either label.

- *The corollary to this being, "He who dies with the most toys wins".*

As it turns out, neither the OPML, nor the "me first, my toy" ideas are from God. In fact, both of these myopic misfortunes of mayhem run counter to the lesson that Elohim gave to Adam & Eve about the nature of work, and about the importance of looking out for the dignity of even the "least of" your most annoying neighbors BEFORE he turned their sorrowful souls out into the world to REPAIR what they had broken through *Tikkum Olam*.

What Cain missed was that:

- *MERCY is the KEY to EVERYTHING*

And anything that runs counter to MERCY is just PLAIN WRONG, because thinking that anything less than Peace will get you something more than Happiness is pure insanity born of an upside-down view of reality that can barely see beyond its own nose let alone into the eyes of The Golden Creative Promise of **FOREVER**!

This is why the first step of the Peacemaker toward being *The Infinity of Happiness Each of Us Was Always Meant To Be* is to turn the Pyramidal thinking of OPML on its head, and to help others who are so FUDS-crazy that they are constantly knocking everybody else "down the ladder" to see that the "more excellent way" St. Paul talks about with The Corinthians is a Way of Being which places the premiums in life on being the most vulnerable, and the most supportive member of the team, to take the hits, and to always "eat last," so that all of the others might have life, and have it more abundantly.

This is the essential wisdom of *The Agility of Grace, in fact, this is what Jesus said of himself, and then backed it up by literally giving us HIS BODY to eat, so that we would have life, even the life of* **FOREVER!**

## Allowing The Transfiguration to Happen -- The Kingdom Come

It was literally on The Day of the Feast of the Transfiguration 2017, the very day of my certification as a Certified Agile Leader, that the fragmented pieces of my life aligned.

As we neared the end our last day, we did a literature review, and capability mapping exercise to help us better follow the "me to we" community forming mechanism that Agile management methods enable, and all other pyramidal management forms either inhibit, or directly oppose. Then I turned the chart we were working on sideways, and it aligned perfectly with the Memory Castle my continued prayers of The Rosary had built in my sustainably renewing mind.

At that point, everything aligned as my mind's eye was illuminated with the picture collage I had put together on my living room wall, and it's golden staircase of the Eucharist climbing up to the Joy of **FOREVER!** Not long after this, in subsequent contemplative prayers as I passed through the vignette of the third Third Luminous Mystery (The Proclamation of The Kingdom of Heaven Come to Earth) that the full Wisdom of the Rosary came flooding in…

- *The Kingdom of God is NOTHING BUT MERCY!*

## MERCY is BOTH the KEY, and THE ENTIRE SUBSTANCE of THE KINGDOM OF HEAVEN.

As the goat path tells us, NON-MERCY shall never, ever be a part of anything that has to do with **FOREVER;** NON-MERCY ISN'T ANYTHING AT ALL, and "for-never" shall be THE SELF-DISSIPATING FOOD OF HELL.

Another thing that emerged to me in my subsequent contemplations was a fleck of wisdom indicating for us that the Rosary is actually a carefully constructed map for community building, and helps us understand the mind of Elohim, The Ever-Existing, Uncreated, Eternal Community of Being, an understanding that has been further enhanced. As such, I have been taken to ever-deeper levels of practical guidance that has led me to add a row BELOW the other four rows to help remind us of the "Glimmering" Mysteries from the Hebraic Scriptures that pre-date the Annunciation.

From this, and from a careful cross-reading of the literature surrounding the Agility management movement, and its related disciplines that focus on the conservation, and celebration of Grace as the primordial engine for improving productivity through creative community building, *The Little Mustard Seed Starter Pack Trilogy* (available at LMSSPT.com, and accessible **FREE** for Knindle Unlimited Subscriber), MERCIPALOOZA.com, LMSFNetwork.com, and even what has now emerged as BE-A-PEACEMAKER.COM.

All of this because I finally stopped *Resisting Happiness* as Matthew Kelly has expounded in his work by the same name, joined the Catholic Faith tradition, started praying the Rosary regularly, as my God-father Steve, the Dominican preacher insisted, and allowed HE-WHO-WAS-AND-IS-AND-IS-TO-COME to BE the change in me that has helped to move me toward being an Infinity of Happiness (or The Happy Gardener, as Peter Green, my guide to CAL Certification enlightenment noted), indeed, The Infinity of Happiness I was always meant to BE.

This is why, as an Agility Coach, I insist that all of our pyramids be turned right-side-up at the beginning of any transformation attempt, so that they can become the planters for growing the healing trees of the Garden of The Agility of Grace we shall grow together as we learn to be still, and be part of each other's lives together, rather than continuing to be the pyramidal co-opting competitors in a contextual grid that isn't even big enough for two people (cf Adam & Eve, and Cain & Able), let alone a whole team. And the Cain & Able story is why I insist that the word "BOSS" be banned from our vocabulary, just like it was before Cain broke Abels head "Like a Boss", just like it was before we broke The Universe by Adam's breaking Eden, simply because he wanted to be The Boss of "don't even touch that..."
**FOREVER!**

## Trusting The Agility of Grace – Make Your Work Child's Play Again

Once things are right-side up again, the rest is fairly natural, if...

If we follow Jesus's instructions to become a child again, and find that Little Mustard Seed of faith he gave to us on the day we were born, and sucked in our first ghastly breath, and cried for help... and in doing so invoked His Grace into our lives.

This literally makes adapting to the Agile management style, living according to the practice, and the pattern of The Peacemaker, and finding the Dignity in our work a matter of "child's play" as we learn again what we knew when we were young, that life truly is meant to be a Party for Mercy's Sake, Each & Every Day! And that anything less than that, as Matthew 25 reminds us, is less than nothing at all.

You can start by browsing over to LMSSPT.com, reading the poems to your children, or your other significant others before bed, when they wake, and as they burst out to start their day.

**AND…Then use the blank spaces in the workbook pages to literally use The Agility of Grace to turn the walls around you into bridges to the future.**

Then itis just a matter of Story Time, Arts & Crafts, a little Modern Dance, some Show & Tell, and some Retrospective Q&A… ALL in the spirit of celebrating our fellow artistic collaborators, and our waiting neighbors for Mercy's Sake, as you shall see below.

And lets get one thing straight before we go there…

Don't get stuck in the quagmire of the never-ending story, don't wait until you have the perfect text, because The Agility of Grace is all about DELIVERY…specifically the delivery of impact toward The Ultimate Happiness of Our Neighbors. And delivery does not happen unless we stop telling each other stories, and start DOING SOMETHING to MAKE SOMETHING to BE REAL!!!

Do remember also, that The Agility of Grace gives us access to ALL of the possibilities the Universe has to offer us, because the root of Agility is HARD SCIENCE.

As such, working with Agility DOES indeed produce the LOVE, based on truth, and not sales puffing, that leads us down the path to The Happiness of Graceful Delivery, and toward an eternity of Peaceful Being.

There is, however, NOTING starry-eyed, or theoretical, or sentimental about it. Because TRUE LOVE is not starry-eyed, TRUE LOVE offers itself as the food of TRUTH, even if that food is served from ground-level, or even hanging from a Tree of Death.

The Agility of Grace is HARD SCIENCE that is meant to deal with the harsh realities of both our real scarcities, and the OPML pomposity we must wade through each, and every day to eke out one more drop of the healing elixir of Mercy for our Neighbors, because The Grace of Agility originates, and is meted out by The Original Scientist, The One who engineered The Universe, and then hung himself out to dry for us at his own, infinite expense… SO WITH THE AGILITY OF GRACE, THERE IS NO PLACE TO RUN… & NO PLACE TO HIDE.

If you choose. to accept the invitation to ENGAGE, you will either learn to BE THE DOING OF MERCY, or you will BE NO MORE in the Garden, and in either case, you shall be a much better person for it, because, in one way or another, the truth will always set you free.

So, as the textbooks say, "Trust the process." And, in all honesty, you will learn to trust in Elohim…

**FOREVER**!

**Instrument of Peace** — *The Saint Francis Prayer*

Lord, make me an instrument of your peace:
where there is hatred, let me sow love;
where there is injury, pardon;
where there is doubt, faith;
where there is despair, hope;
where there is darkness, light;
where there is sadness, joy.

***O divine Master, grant that I may not
so much seek to be consoled as to console,***
to be understood as to understand,
to be loved as to LOVE.
For it is in giving that we receive,
it is in pardoning that we are pardoned,
and it is in dying that we are born to eternal life.
Amen.

## THE AGILITY OF GRACE

And understanding, indeed, that all of BEING, is all about QUESTIONS, and about the Shared Stories that result (as long as we don't lose ourselves in the weeds of the stories, and die of non-delivery of the harvesting of them).

To keep the purpose of your story telling at the front of your mind, just remember the acronym **ICED**:

- *IMPACT*
- *CONTRIBUTION*
- *ENGAGEMENT*
- *DATA*

And remember that you are dealing with "Amazing AMPed-up ICE", because your stories, and your data analysis is NEVER to be used for the FEAR & REPRISAL that fuel the culture of The FUDS of OPML. INSTEAD the ICE is to be used to max out AUTONOMY (both at the individual, and collaboration group level), MASTERY, and PURPOSE…also known as the WHAT, the HOW, and the WHY of being.

For a good overview of how to build a culture using The Agility of Grace, check out the Spotify Vimeos at:

Part 1:  https://vimeo.com/85490944?ref=em-share

Part 2:  https://vimeo.com/94950270?ref=em-share

For more on What, How & Finding Your Why, pick up *Find Your Why* by Simon Sinek, at:
https://www.amazon.com/Find-Your-Why-Practical-Discovering-ebook/dp/B01CZCW3ZA/

Because…
#1 It is an excellent book that I would have written myself, had it not existed already, and…
#2 It contains both Agile principles, and principles of Peaceful Being (of nesting where you are bent to be)

As such, I will not recreate a well made wheel.

Once you have done the ground work, make sure that you answer all of the questions below in a word, "religiously", otherwise you will do nothing but spin your wheels, and sub-optimize whatever you touch.  And plan to do all of them every day in one way, or another somewhere in your enterprise by someone, or another (or even several others), because The Agility of Grace is a full-contact sport that either everybody plays, from the tip of the inverted pyramid, to the tops of the leaves of the tree of Agility that emerges through our uniquely creative collaborative contributions, and our undying commitment to the delivery of Our Ultimate Happens to Our neighbors… OR a game that nobody plays at ALL for LESS THAN NOTHING AT ALL.

**Always remember that there is always more than one 'i" in Agility.**

It is ESSENTIAL that of EVERYONE BE involved, and that EVERYONE perceives The Agility of Grace as the ONLY way to BE!

This is full metal Agility for the largest enterprises on Earth (including the One, Holy, Catholic, and Apostolic Church), and for those who are serious about changing their Way of Being.  IF YOU ARE NOT SERIOUS ABOUT DOING THIS TO ITS FULLEST EXTENT…

DO SOMETHING ELSE.

You, and everbody who works with you will be happier.

OTHERWISE… HAVE FUN & GET ON YOUR WAY!!!

**And keep in mind as you go, we ARE dancing toward a PARTY at the END OF TIME for MERCY'S SAKE after all (pun intended).**

And please note: The Impact Levels below have been designed so that you can always add levels with higher numbers (below the root, instead of impacting the tree above) as you find more general reasons to organize the stories in to categories with more general purposes. So, there is no need to add levels below #1 (or up into the trunk of your tree).

**IMPACT LEVEL 6: OPPORTUNISTIC Stories Celebrating Our Uniquely Creative Contributions WE COULD SCHEDULE FOR DELIVERY AT ANY TIME to Make a Positive Impact Toward the Ultimate Happiness of Our Neighbors**

Same questions as IMPACT 3.

**IMPACT LEVEL 5: STRATEGIC Stories Celebrating Our Uniquely Creative Contributions WE COULD DELIVER in the next 3 to 5 YEARS to Make a Positive Impact Toward the Ultimate Happiness of Our Neighbors**

Same questions as IMPACT 3.

**IMPACT LEVEL 4: TACTICAL Stories Celebrating Our Uniquely Creative Contributions WE COULD DELIVER in the NEXT YEAR to Make a Positive Impact Toward the Ultimate Happiness of Our Neighbors**

Same questions as IMPACT 3.

**IMPACT LEVEL 3: EPIC Stories Celebrating Our Uniquely Creative Contributions WE COULD DELIVER in the NEXT QUARTER to Make a Positive Impact Toward the Ultimate Happiness of Our Neighbors**

What are all of the packages of the uniquely creative contributions we could deliver to make a positive impact toward the Ultimate Happiness of Our Neighbors?

Who could we invite to celebrate with us as collaborating contributors?

What application of Machine-Platform-Crowd could we employ to maximize the contribution of each & every contributor each & every day?

**IMPACT LEVEL 2: IMMEDIATE Stories Celebrating Our Uniquely Creative Contributions WE PLAN TO Deliver in the NEXT FORTNIGHT to Make a Positive Impact Toward the Ultimate Happiness of Our Neighbors**

In the next fortnight, what is the next package of uniquely creative contributions we want to be able to deliver to Our Neighbors to make a positive impact toward their Ultimate Happiness?

Who do we want to be able to invite to celebrate with us as a collaborating contributors?

What application of Machine-Platform-Crowd do we want to be able to employ to maximize the contribution of each & every contributor each & every day?

**IMPACT LEVEL 1: DAILY Stories Celebrating Our Uniquely Creative Contributions WE HAVE DELIVERED to Make a Positive Impact Toward the Ultimate Happiness of Our Neighbors**

For each team member... Since last we met, what uniquely creative contribution have you delivered toward the Ultimate Happiness of Our Neighbors which both Your Collaborators & Our Neighbors would agree has been demonstrated to be done?

Who do you wish to celebrate now as a collaborating contributor in this delivery?

What application of Machine-Platform-Crowd have you employed to maximize the contribution of each & every contributor?

**CONTRIBUTION: DAILY Stories Celebrating Our Uniquely Creative Contributions WE ARE DELIVERING to Make a Positive Impact Toward the Ultimate Happiness of Our Neighbors**

Today, what is the next uniquely creative contribution toward the Ultimate Happiness of Our Neighbors you would like to be able to deliver & to demonstrate as done?

With whom would you like to be able to celebrate with as a collaborating contributor in this delivery?

What application of Machine-Platform-Crowd would you like to be able to employ to maximize the contribution of each & every contributor each & every day?

**ENGAGEMENT: DAILY Stories of Our Uniquely Creative Contributions WE MUST CELEBRATE FOR MERCY'S SAKE TO BE ABLE TO DELIVER a Positive Impact Toward the Ultimate Happiness of Our Neighbors in spite of our blocking challenges**

Today, what is blocking you from demonstrating & celebrating the delivery of your uniquely creative contribution as done?

Today, with whom would you like to be able to collaborate, so that, together, you can make forward progress toward celebrating your delivery as done?

What application of Machine-Platform-Crowd would you like to be able to employ to maximize the contribution of each & every contributor today?

**DATA DISCOVERY:** Questions of Glimmering, Discovery, Revelation, Retrospection & Expansion of Context to be asked BEFORE crossing every IMPACT THRESHOLD, and DAILY, AS NECESSARY, both to detect the presence of any Dodecahedral Tesseracts of Grace (aka needs for the expansion of context to bring us back to a state of Peaceful Prodcutivity) that have emerged, and to address the new context of any that cascade down the Delivery Tree. (cf. *Be Mindful, Little Mustard Seed* by Grant William Shull @ LMSSPT.com, *The Art of Possibility* by Zander & Zander)

### Celebrations of Our Neighbors
Who are our Our Neighbors?

What "networks of caring" do they form by connecting with each other?

### Celebrations of Our Collaborators
Who are Our Collaborators?

What "networks of delivery" do we form by connecting with each other?

### Celebrations of The MPC
What are the Machine-Platform-Crowd (MPC) components we want to be able to employ overall to align both Our Collaborators & Our Tools into a web of machine-assisted humans as a collaborative backbone enabling us to celebrate our deliveries for maximum, balanced overall effectiveness, efficiency, impact toward happiness, and return of grace with respect regard to the quality, speed, price, and value of our delivery?

For each uniquely creative contribution demonstrated to be done?

Of each package?

Of specifically nested taxonomies?

For deliveries not yet done, and abandoned for each of the preceding categories?

Overall?

What is the sequencing that webs both our collaborators, and our MPC components together to form the backbone of our Agility of Grace given the comparative collaborative advantage of each?

### The Solemnity of The Definitions of Done — Neighbor Perspective

What will Our Neighbors need to experience to agree that a delivery of a uniquely creative contribution has been demonstrated to be done?

Of each package?

Of specifically nested taxonomies?

Of deliveries not yet done for each of the preceding categories?

Overall?

### The Solemnity of The Definitions of Done — Collaborator Perspective

What will each collaborator need to experience to agree that a delivery of a uniquely creative contribution has been demonstrated to be done?

Of each package?

Of specifically nested taxonomies?

For deliveries not yet done for each of the preceding categories?

Overall?

### Celebrations of The Perception of Value — Neighbor Perspective

From the perspective of Our Neighbors, what value has each uniquely creative contribution delivered toward their Ultimate Happiness?

For each package?

For specifically nested taxonomies?

For deliveries not yet done, and abandoned for each of the preceding categories?

Overall?

### **The Solemnity of The Expenditures of Grace**
What has been Our Total Expenditure of Grace for each uniquely creative contribution?

For each package?

For specifically nested taxonomies?

For deliveries not yet done, and abandoned for each of the preceding categories?

Overall?

### **Celebrations of The Return of Grace**
From the perspective of Our Collaborators, what has been our Return of Grace from Our Neighbors for each uniquely creative contribution?

For each package?

For specifically nested taxonomies?

For deliveries not yet done, and abandoned for each of the preceding categories?

Overall?

### **Celebrations of The Mysteries Grace**
What unexpected returns of Grace have we experienced for each uniquely creative contribution?

For each package?

For specifically nested taxonomies?

For deliveries not yet done, and abandoned for each of the preceding categories?

Overall?

### *Celebrations for Mercy's Sake*
What Offerings of Mercy should be celebrated for each uniquely creative contribution?

For each package?

For specifically nested taxonomies?

For deliveries not yet done, and abandoned for each of the preceding categories?

Overall?

### *Celebrations of Truth, Beauty & Goodness*
What examples of truth, and beauty, and goodness should be celebrated for each uniquely creative contribution?

For each package?

For specifically nested taxonomies?

For deliveries not yet done, and abandoned for each of the preceding categories?

Overall?

### *Celebration of The Agility of Grace*
What new contexts of Grace were created for each uniquely creative contribution?

For each package?

For specifically nested taxonomies?

For deliveries not yet done, and abandoned for each of the preceding categories?

Overall?

### *The Solemnity of The New Contexts of The Agility of Grace*

Into what new contexts of Grace would we like to be able to expand the celebration of our collaboration based on our experiences delivering each uniquely creative contribution so far?

Each package?

Specifically nested taxonomies?

Deliveries not yet done, and abandoned for each of the preceding categories?

Overall?

**As You May Have Noticed -- Grace is Grace is Grace.**

The Grace found in The Practice of The Last Planner that is at the heart of all forms Agility in one way or another, is he who truly holds the commercial practices of Agility together by the power of LOVE, for HE IS the same collaborative "glue" of The Agility of Grace who gives daily birth to Mercy among us, and holds us together to accomplish all successful deliveries toward The Ultimate Happiness of Our Neighbors, because he is, indeed, and in deed, the same Holy Spirit of Grace who continually, and super-abundantly cascades down upon us like a never-ending dewfall, blessing our Eucharistic living patterns, and empowering us to implement The Merciful Practice of *The Least of These* found in Matthew 25, regardless of whether we have direct commercial interest in the outcomes or not.

## Therefore, Let Us Be Resolved:

To sustainably expand The Happiness demonstrated by the ever-expanding capability context of our webbed collaborative delivery backbone which we, in turn seek to sustainably expand as our employment of The Agility of Grace for sustainably delivering our ever-expanding goodwill to our neighbors, opportunistically packaged as a continually expanding suite of our uniquely creative contributions designed to deliver the maximum positive impact toward The Ultimate Happiness of Our Neighbors, and, by reflexive extension through The Super-Abundant Return of Our Grace toward Our Ultimate Happiness as well.  Let us further resolve to "be still" while listen to the voice of others to understand before being understood, so that the "How" & "Why" & "What Next" of this process shall be made known to us as we continually share the stories of our Hopes, and Dreams, together, in the context of The Agility of Grace, and Party Together for Mercy's Sake in the face of bold, and practically bounded, yet boundlessly opportunistic scientific experiments that help us To Believe We Can Dare to Do What We Hope to Dream Come True.

And May the LORD God of Hosts have Mercy on Our Sorrowful Souls as we ENGAGE in the Enterprise of Love,
**FOREVER**!

Amen.

# The Tools & Texts of The Peacemaker

## Starter List

To help you focus your thoughts about "Delivering Happiness" — *Mother Teresa's Prescription* by Paul A. Wright, MD.

https://www.amazon.com/Mother-Teresas-Prescription-Finding-Happiness-ebook/dp/B002WJI8HO/

For our virtual classroom/workroom, we will use:

newrow.com

After you go to BE-A-PEACEMAKER.COM and JOIN the Little Mustard Seed MERCIPALOOZA FOREVER Corp (The LMSMFC), you will be sent a link to join our work in a specific room. At most, there will be 25 of us in any one room at any one time.

Each room will also have its own trello.com board, so that we can learn together by working.

Again, once you JOIN THE **MERCIPALOOZA FOREVER CORP**, you will receive a link to your team's creative collaboration board.

Go to LMSSPT.com, to get the Little Mustard Seed Trilogy Starter Pack

And do think very deeply about accepting my invitation to get a Kindle Unlimited subscription (if you haven't yet), and read through the *Little Mustard Seed Starter Pack Trilogy* on-line, and think of where you want to allocate space for walls that we will turn into bridges to the future (if, that is you want something physical beyond Trello).

Whether you are joining to help your business, or not, the following are either essential, or tantamount to being essential, so, as *Hermione of Hogwarts* would say, "Didn't You Do Your Reading":

- *Pick up* The E-myth *by Michael E. Gerber, and think about planning your global biz from the beginning. (Who else are you going to need as you grow, and how can you segment their roles in the grand distribution web of Happiness you will build?)*

https://www.amazon.com/Myth-Revisited-Small-Businesses-About-ebook/dp/B000RO9VJK/

- *Pick up The Art of Possibility by Zander & Zander (or better yet, get the audio version and enjoy listening to Ben, and Rosamund speak, which alone is worth the price of admission), and "give yourself an 'A' for life" by writing a letter to St. Peter as your apology for your life at the pearly gates. Remember, "being still" has nothing in common with being either unengaged, or completely inert. No Neem Trees, no navels, and no idle gazing, please!*

https://www.amazon.com/Art-Possibility-Transforming-Professional-Personal-ebook/dp/B00N1KJ76E/

**Audio**: https://www.amazon.com/Art-Possibility-Transforming-Professional-Personal/dp/B004HY9254/

- *Matthew Kelly's Resisting Happiness.*

https://www.amazon.com/Resisting-Happiness-Matthew-Kelly-ebook/dp/B01JNM8ADY/

- *An explanation of The Memorare, in the context of a man who met Mary much as I did at my Baptism (which is a story that is best told face-to-face in our workroom). The Conversion of St. Alphonse Ratisbonne...*

https://www.tfp.org/the-conversion-of-alphonse-ratisbonne/

- *The Memorare*

https://www.ourladyswarriors.org/prayer/memorare.htm

Prayed 100 times by Count de La Ferronays at the request of Baron Thèodore de Bussières, "The Bold", for the conversion of St. Alphonse Ratisbonne perhaps causing Ferronays' death.

You may also be interested in the life of St. Padre Pío, who had an ongoing conversation with Our Lady, and experienced life outside of space-time as well.

http://catholicsaints.info/saint-padre-pio/

- *As already noted, pick up a copy of Find Your Why by Simon Sinek. And begin to tell stories of what impact you want to have with what you are delivering now, and whatever comes after it, in the world as part of your distribution of Happiness. We shall use these stories to focus on on your big purpose (your "Why") is. I would be especially interested in stories that tell what is connected to any reoccurring words that pop up as you begin to tell your stories to yourself in your life history, in your present experience, and in your hopes & dreams for the future. [You also might be interested in the works of Henry David Thoreau.]*

https://www.amazon.com/Find-Your-Why-Practical-Discovering-ebook/dp/B01CZCW3ZA/

- *Also begin to tell (aka write down) stories [Right now, I cannot __do what?__, because __what is blocking the way?__ is preventing my forward progress, if I could ___do what?*

__, I would be able to __do what?___, so that I could __deliver what impact?___.] of what is blocking your way in the context of your current trial, and what you can do to GO THROUGH the middle of it with the most truth, beauty, and goodwill intact, who you need to help you, and what must be done next, and next, and next to remove each blocker. Try not to think beyond three "best next things".

And if Mary catches your eye in all of this, then *33 Days to Morning Glory* by Michael E. Gaitley will really jumpstart your life… (and it just might blow all the doors off as were mine). This book is ultimately the reason that I am writing to you now…

This is why I care.

This is The Main Gateway TO…
**FOREVER!**

https://www.amazon.com/Days-Morning-Glory-Do-Yourself-ebook/dp/B00DJDZMXK/

Spotify Culture Vimeos:

Part 1:  https://vimeo.com/85490944?ref=em-share

Part 2:  https://vimeo.com/94950270?ref=em-share

*Agile Product Ownership in a Nutshell* by Henrik Kniberg
(POs is standard Agile parlance for what we will refer to as Product Stewards):

https://youtu.be/502ILHjX9EE

*Scrum by The Book* by Per Beining (The same kinds of terminology substitution will be necessary here…we have made the shift to "delivery" as the goal, not development, and stewardship, instead of ownership):

https://www.youtube.com/watch?v=TYCeGy69mLE

*Learn agile estimation in 10 minutes* by David Griffiths

https://www.youtube.com/watch?v=Hwu438QSb_g

*The Agile Manifesto* (where you see "software" related terms, think generically "product" (aka something you can deliver, even if it is a show, experience, or service).

http://agilemanifesto.org

*The Agile Principles* (same here for "software" related terms)
http://agilemanifesto.org/principles.html

Adapt both of the above for the purpose of delivering what your uniquely contribute toward the Happiness of YOUR Neighbors. For "service oriented" enterprises, it may help to think of working software, as a packaged, scripted, and rehearsed performance event with the actual product as the "take-away" for an audience.

**ESSENTIAL!!!** When you line up a product steward (many times for small business owners, this is your spouse) you, and your steward must be vision-linked. So, make sure you focus on successful transfer of vision now, and keep revisiting, EVERY DAY at first, and then at least EVERY TWO WEKS in retro to stay aligned.

Notice the value curve in the video above looks like Kuhn's paradigm theory s-curve with the declining tail cut off. The next curve starts around where the tail cut is, drops, and then rises higher, that's why a leap of faith to the next curve from the cut produces maximum value output.

**I used this one to help turn IBM into <u>the largest "Agile at Scale" enterprise on the face of the Earth</u>, and as a byproduct help to crate Cynefin:**

- *The Structure of Scientific Revolutions: 50th Anniversary Edition* by Thomas S. Kuhn

https://www.amazon.com/Structure-Scientific-Revolutions-50th-Anniversary-ebook/dp/B007USH7J2/

**REMEMBER <u>NO LYING</u> = Disclosure, Transparency, Servant Leadership, and aiming for the Highest Purpose Possible** (and everyone on the team needs to observe these practices at all times with…No Fear & No Reprisals…so Failures must be met with Mercy, and Goodwill to repair/improve, not scorn, and condemnation, and vilification [the Law killeth, but the Spirit giveth life] — this is part of "leading from any chair" and learning to dance naked in public (Zander & Zander).

Some other cool resources, and context builders…

- *The Second Machine* Age by Brynjolfsson & McAfee

https://www.amazon.com/Second-Machine-Age-Prosperity-Technologies-ebook/dp/B00D97HPQI/

- *Machine Platform Crowd* by Brynjolfsson & McAfee

https://www.amazon.com/Machine-Platform-Crowd-Harnessing-Digital-ebook/dp/B01MAWT25I/

- *Aristotle's Poetics* by Aristotle
https://www.amazon.com/Poetics-Penguin-Classics-Aristotle-ebook/dp/B002RI92L6/

- *How to Convince Them in 90 Seconds or Less* by Nicholas Boothman

- *First They Came…*
    By Pastor Martin Niemöller
    https://en.wikipedia.org/wiki/First_they_came_

- *Man in Search of Meaning* by Viktor Frankl pdf… (this was a BIG game changer for me)
    https://ediscipinas.usp.br/pluginfile.php/3403095/mod_resource/content/1/56ViktorFrankl_Mans%20Search.pdf

    Note that Dr. Frankl developed an entire therapy around the second significance of the Greek word *Logos* (translated "The Word" in St. John's Gospel, Chapter 1)

    The first significance of *Logos* is "the symbol" or "the pointer"…

    The third is "the realization" (which the Gospels, especially Matthew 25 [Mother Teresa's Favorite] describe as Mercy)…

    And the forth is BECOMING MERCY for others as we allow the Transubstantiation of the Host of the Eucharist become our Transubstantiation even now, even here on this face of This Earth.

You will find a discussion of the first three significances in *The Handbook of Catholic Apologetics: Reasoned Answers to Questions of Faith* by Kreeft & Tacelli

https://www.amazon.com/Handbook-Catholic-Apologetics-Reasoned-Questions-ebook-dp-B01F9GV8H8/dp/B01F9GV8H8/

You will find a discussion of the forth in very few place, here and at BE-A-PEACEMAKER.COM are a couple of maybe a handful.

Another place where this discipline is taught is in The Cloud of the Unknowing by Anonymous written sometime in the Middle Ages. Make sure you have tight elastic on your socks for this one:

https://www.amazon.com/Cloud-Unknowing/dp/1542987997

And if you like dystopian science-fiction that tells tales of Anti-Agility Margaret Atwood has you covered (she's the bees knees on this subject)
- The *Maddaddam Trilogy*

https://www.amazon.com/gp/product/B0749R84MD/

Finally, if you do decide to:

BE-A-PEACEMAKER.COM

You will find one of our sales support resources there, namely, "The Pattern of The Peacemaker".

This resource is intended to be an introduction for you into the new new work room you have joined as a member of "The Little Mustard Seed **MERCIPALOOZA FOREVER CORP.**"

The current version of this resource is duplicated here along with the remapping of some of the resources listed above, so that you can see the value in joining **THE LMSFMC**…

## The Pattern of A Peacemaker

Please review the overview presentation by Grant William Shull at BE-A-PEACEMAKER.COM before reviewing the information below. This is intended as a guide to the activities & resources that will color our engagement in The Agility of Grace.

As you shall see, it is quite bony, and well thought out, as far as the framework for our dreaming, learning, collaborating, and delivery of Happiness to our Neighbors.

The dreams that you bring, the impacts you want to make, the contributions you can make, and the additional collaborators you can engage in our shared work together makes the meat.

Please note: Our common Team Board at trello.com can function as one single roadmap for one single work stream we all work on, or as 24 different streams.

Under the principle that we have not been brought together by merely random events, but we have a purpose for being here together that requires our shared action, we shall let the Holy Spirit of All Agility & Grace lead us, and The VOX shall trust him in his leading.

***Everybody Meet Every Day with The VOX of Mercy for a Happy Hour Shot***
**Be Ready for Your Shot at Show & Tell Time — Ding, Done, Doing & Dan't:**
Guiding Resources: *The Little Mustard Seed Starter Pack Trilogy* & BE-A-PEACEMAKER.COM from LMSSPT.COM by Grant William Shull; *Spotify Culture of Innovation Part 1*: https://vimeo.com/85490944?ref=em-share; *Spotify Culture of Innovation Part 2*: https://vimeo.com/94950270?ref=em-share; The Agile Manifesto (where you see "software" related terms, think generically "product" (aka something you can deliver, even if it is a show, experience, or service)… http://agilemanifesto.org;The Agile Principles (same here for "software" related terms) http://agilemanifesto.org/principles.html; *Agile Product Ownership in a Nutshell* (POs is standard Agile parlance for what we will refer to as Delivery Stewards): https://youtu.be/502ILHjX9EE; *Scrum by The Book* by Per Beining (The same kinds of terminology substitution will be necessary here…we have made the shift to "delivery" as the goal, not development, and stewardship, instead of ownership): https://www.youtube.com/watch?v=TYCeGy69mLE

- Be Online on Time in the Team Room at NewRow.com
- BE REAL
- BE BRIEF
- AND PASS THE BATTON
- Have Your trello.com cards updated before beginning
- Celebrate What You Have Done Since Your Last Time in the Vox
- Demonstrate The Impact of What You Have Done Since Your Last Time in the Vox
- Tell Your Team What You Are Doing TODAY
- Ensure trello.com reflects any updates
- Tell Your Team What is Blocking Your Progress RIGHT NOW
- Post a Blocker on trello.com, if it is not already there

***Everybody Meet Every Day with Your Team — Post VOX***
**Use the Whole Happy Hour (Start of VOX Plus 3 hours)**
Guiding Resources: *The Art of Possibility* by Zander & Zander

- Stay Online in the Team Room at NewRow.com
- BE REAL
- BE MERCIFUL
- AND BE KIND
- Elaborate Your Stories of Celebration
- Deeply Demonstrate What You Have Done
- Share Your Stories of Blockers
- Share Your Stories of Overcoming
- Volunteer to Help Others
- Collaborate to Get Everyone to Both Their & Our Done Together
- Update Your trello.com Cards Collaboratively Throughout Your Work Session

***Your First Six Weeks with The VOX***
**Deep Retrospection: Find Your Why**
Guiding Resources: *The Little Mustard Seed Starter Pack Trilogy* & BE-A-PEACEMAKER.COM from LMSSPT.COM by Grant William Shull; *Find Your Why* by Simon Sinek; *Resisting Happiness* by Matthew Kelly; *Mother Teresa's Prescription* by by Paul A. Wright, M.D.; *Aristotle's Poetics* by Aristotle; One-Minute Aquinas by Kevin Vost; The

Catechistic Resources downloadable from our Team Room; *Man in Search of Meaning* by Viktor Frankl pdf... (this was a game changer for me) https://ediscipinas.usp.br/pluginfile.php/3403095/mod_resource/content/1/56ViktorFrankl_Mans%20Search.pdf

- Post on Team Board at trello.com:
- BE REAL
- Stories of Impact
- As ... when I was ... I was able to ...; as a result I felt that I ...
- As ... when I was ..., ... my ... did something that helped me, particularly this person ...; as a result I felt that I ...
- As ... a ... I observed that when ... was ..., ... our ... did something that helped us, particularly this person ...; as a result I felt that I ...
- As ... a ... I want to be able to increase the impact of what I do by ..., so that ...
- As ... a ... I believe we could increase our impact together if we ..., so that ...
- Statement of Purpose
- As ... a ... It is my purpose to ... so that ...
- To Do in Team Room — Post VOX
- BE REAL
- Share Your Stories
- Help Others
- Commend Others
- Update Your trello.com Cards Continuously & Collaboratively Throughout Your Work Session

### *Your Second Six Weeks with The VOX*
**Deep Dreaming: Dream Your Mission**
Guiding Resources: Books from LMSSPT.COM by Grant William Shull; *Find Your Why* by Simon Sinek; *Resisting Happiness* by Matthew Kelly; *Mother Teresa's Prescription* by by Paul A. Wright, M.D.

- Post on Team Board at trello.com:
- Stories of Your Desire to Make a Meaningful Contribution
- As ... a ... I want to be able to ... so that ...
- Stories of Your Existing Collaborative Advantage Potential
- As ... a ... I can ... so that ...
- Stories of Your Desired Collaborative Advantages
- As ... a ... I need help to ... so that ...
- Stories of Your Blockers
- As ... a ... I fear that I will not be able to ... because ...
- As ... a ... I doubt that I will be able to ... because ...
- As ... a ... I am uncertain that I will be able to ... because ...
- As ... a ... I am sad that I will not be able to ... because ...
- As ... a ... I am ashamed that I am not able to ... because ...
- Update Your trello.com Cards Collaboratively Throughout Your Work Sessions Together
- To Do in Team Room — Post VOX
- Share Your Stories
- Help Others
- Commend Others
- Update Your trello.com Cards Continuously & Collaboratively Throughout Your Work Session

*Your Third Six Weeks with The VOX*
**Deep Analysis: Believe Your Mission in Action**
Guiding Resources: Books from LMSSPT.COM by Grant William Shull; *The Art of Possibility* by Zander & Zander; Agile at Scale, Harvard Business Review, May-June 2018 (https://hbr.org/2018/05/agile-at-scale); *The Structure of Scientific Revolutions: 50th Anniversary Edition* by Thomas S. Kuhn; *The Second Machine Age* by Brynjolfsson & McAfee; *Machine Platform Crowd* by Brynjolfsson & McAfee; *Learn agile estimation in 10 minutes* by David Griffiths: https://www.youtube.com/watch?v=Hwu438QSb_g; *The E-myth* by Michael E. Gerber

- Drill Down into Your Dreams with Realizable Actions of Delivery
- Always add stories that speak about the One-Button Automation of anything that you dream into Action, even if you need to put them on the back burner by writing corresponding stories of blockers immediately… It is better to have these burins as candles on the table, than hidden in a corner
- Determine what the BEST-NEXT stories to deliver are
- Post on Team Board at trello.com:
- Stories of Your Delivery
- As … a … I want to be able to deliver … to our neighbors so that …
- As … a … I want to be able to deliver … for our neighbors so that …
- As … a … I can contribute to the delivery of … by … so that …
- Stories of Your Existing Collaborative Delivery Advantage Potential
- As … a … I can help to deliver … by … so that …
- Stories of Your Desired Collaborative Delivery Advantages
- As … a … I need help in delivering …, particularly I need help … so that …
- Stories of Your Delivery Blockers
- As … a … I fear that I will not be able to deliver … because …
- As … a … I doubt that I will be able to deliver … because …
- As … a … I am uncertain that I will be able to deliver … because …
- As … a … I am sad that I will not be able to deliver … because …
- As … a … I am ashamed that I am not able to deliver … because …
- As a team … I … a … believe that we could deliver … so that …
- To Do in Team Room — Post VOX
- Share Your Stories
- Help Others
- Commend Others
- Update Your trello.com Cards Continuously & Collaboratively Throughout Your Work Session

*Your Forth Six Weeks with The VOX*
**Deep Data: Make Demonstration Templates**
Guiding Resources: *The Little Mustard Seed Starter Pack Trilogy* & BE-A-PEACEMAKER.COM from LMSSPT.COM by Grant William Shull; *The MUSIC Driven No-Update Redaction Engine Pattern for AI* by Grant William Shull; *Enterprise Data Analysis & Design* (aka. The Colonel Method) by Peter P. Jones; *Talk Like Ted* by Carmine Gallo, *Convince Them in 90 Seconds or Less* by Nicholas Boothman

- Make Template Displays To:
- Delineate The Various Audiences to Reach for Various Celebrations

- Ensure Your Neighbors are at least one audience
- Ensure The World is at least one audience
- Delineate The Various Audiences to Reach for Various Demonstrations
- Celebrate the Impact of The Happiness of Your Deliveries
- Demonstrate the Impact of The Happiness of Your Deliveries
- Tell Your Neighbors about The Happiness of Your Deliveries
- Tell The World about The Happiness of Your Deliveries
- Tell Various Audiences About The Happiness of Your Deliveries
- Invite Your Neighbors to Share in The Happiness of Your Deliveries
- Invite The World to Share in The Happiness of Your Deliveries
- Invite Various Audiences to Share in The Happiness of Your Deliveries
- Invite Various Audiences to Participate in The Happiness of The Success of Your Deliveries
- Demonstrate What You Did to Achieve The Happiness of Your Deliveries
- Demonstrate What You Must Yet Do to Achieve Greater Happiness in Your Deliveries
- Demonstrate a Model of The Happiness of Your Deliveries
- Celebrate the Future by Using Adapting Your Model to Project The Increasing Future Happiness of Your Deliveries
- Build Automated Data Structures that will capture data points to create one-button automation of the production of the various Templates defined above
- Automate the Production of The Specific Instances of the Templates

***Every Two Weeks FOREVER: Start a New Sprint with The VOX***
**Sprint: Make it REAL**
*The Little Mustard Seed Starter Pack Trilogy & BE-A-PEACEMAKER.COM* from LMSSPT.COM by Grant William Shull; *Spotify Culture of Innovation Part 1*: https://vimeo.com/85490944?ref=em-share; *Spotify Culture of Innovation Part 2*: https://vimeo.com/94950270?ref=em-share; The Agile Manifesto (where you see "software" related terms, think generically "product" (aka something you can deliver, even if it is a show, experience, or service)… http://agilemanifesto.org; The Agile Principles (same here for "software" related terms) http://agilemanifesto.org/principles.html; *Agile Product Ownership in a Nutshell* by Henrik Kniberg (POs is standard Agile parlance for what we will refer to as Product Stewards): https://youtu.be/502ILHjX9EE; *Scrum by The Book* by Per Beining (The same kinds of terminology substitution will be necessary here…we have made the shift to "delivery" as the goal, not development, and stewardship, instead of ownership): https://www.youtube.com/watch?v=TYCeGy69mLE; *Learn agile estimation in 10 minutes* by David Griffiths: https://www.youtube.com/watch?v=Hwu438QSb_g

- Each & Every Day
- Repeat ALL Deep Tasks at The Sprint Level
- Don't Dive Deep, Just Do The Best Next Thing
- DELIVER
- AND MOVE ON
- If it is not delivered to your Neighbor, it is not done!
- Focus on Delivery
- Fix Everyday Friction
- Tell Stories Celebrating the Elimination of Everyday Friction at trello.com
- As … a …, I am celebrating … a …, when … to the action to … it helped me to …, and helped us all to … so that/because …

- Track Lasting Friction
- Tell Stories for Eliminating Lasting Friction
- As … a …, I have observed that when we … we …, because …
- As … a …, I want us to be able to eliminate friction in our delivery by … so that …

**Call a Time Out for Yourself with The VOX (This can also be done as a team, when the team determines it is necessary)**
**Before Beginning Any New Sprint**
Guiding Resources: *The Little Mustard Seed Starter Pack Trilogy* & BE-A-PEACEMAKER.COM from LMSSPT.COM by Grant William Shull; *Find Your Why* by Simon Sinek; *Resisting Happiness* by Matthew Kelly; *Mother Teresa's Prescription* by by Paul A. Wright, M.D.; *Aristotle's Poetics* by Aristotle; One-Minute Aquinas by Kevin Vost; The Catechistic Resources downloadable from our Team Room; *Man in Search of Meaning* by Viktor Frankl PDF… (this was a game changer for me) https://edisciplinas.usp.br/pluginfile.php/3403095/mod_resource/content/1/56ViktorFrankl_Mans%20Search.pdf

- Take Six Weeks to dive in any Deep Dive Area that needs to be Addressed to help forward progress of all sprints
- It is OK, and very healthy to do this… better to fix what we can see as a recurring risk to success, than to hide from it in the dark, and be blindsided by failure

## AND THAT'S NOT ALL

Once we get to the Classroom/Workroom there will be more.. In fact, there is an entire E-Chatechism and RCIA sequence which I am adapting from Matthew Kelly's latest release for confirmation, and synthesizing for additional adults waiting there for those who choose to JOIN The LMSMFC at:

In the meantime, these should keep you busy.

AND, HOPEFULLY anticipating…
**FOREVER!**

# The Dignity of The Peacemaker

To Labor With & For Autonomy, Mastery & Purpose **Forever**

To realize the dignity of our labor, we must be at peace with the work of our hands even unto mastery for Mercy's Sake:

- *Through what we Deliver with the uniquely creative opus of our hands.*

- *With whom, and with what we collaborate to sustainably deliver our shared opus throughout our lifetime.*

- *And in the contextual cloud of The Agility of Grace, by whom we believe, and into whom we hope to make of us The Delivery of Our Shared Opus of Charity to the ever-expanding delight of Our Neighbors, even unto The Eternal, Golden Fingered Dawn of Our Ultimate Happiness where we may BE Fully & Uniquely Free To Be Autonomously & Ecstatically at Peace with Mercy & with one another, Our Neighbors of Solemnity, Our Block Party Friends of Shared Mercy, The Dignity of Our Oneness of Being, AND The Enduring of…*

**FOREVER.**

Amen

## The Question of the Peacemaker

### Do I Have to be of The Catholic Faith Tradition to Be a Peacemaker?

**NO!**

…not to start with, anyway…
as long as you take MERCY along as YOUR KEY.

**AND…**

*I INVITE YOU TO* **TRY YOUR HARDEST** *TO:*
   BE-A-PEACEMAKER.COM
**REGARDLESS OF:**
   **WHERE YOU HAVE COME FROM**
   **WHAT YOU HAVE LIVED THROUGH, AND**
   **WHAT POSITION YOU HAVE NOW TAKEN UP ON YOUR JOURNEY**

**Because I have been there, and I know how impossible making Mercy work outside of our fully-orbed Messianic tradition is.**

And I know that if you are trying your hardest to be a Peacemaker, we are both doing what we can to Help Mercy Abound wherever we are, or whatever we are doing!

And as Jesus, himself said as he went about His Father's business of helping people to become "ageless children again", and to REMEMBER TO BE the Little Mustard Seeds of faith that can move all the mountains of this world simply by saying a single, solitary word spoken from the heart of **FOREVER**…when the time is right…

Even if that time is when you are hanging on a cross right next to him in the Noonday sun in the heat of the Palestine Spring with a hungry, angry crowd nipping at your heals, and cheering on your death.

As St. Mark puts how Jesus saw the remembering of ourselves not as the OPML strivings to be "the first" or "the best" or "winning" but to become as children, literally to BE The Peacemaking Children of God, simply with a single, solitary fiat of faith:

- *And they came to Capharnaum. And when they were in the house, he asked them: What did you treat of in the way? But they held their peace, for in the way they had disputed among themselves, which of them should be the greatest. And sitting down, he called the twelve, and saith to them: If any man desire to be first, he shall be the last of all, and the minister of all. And taking a child, he set him in the midst of them. Whom when he had embraced, he saith to them: Whosoever shall receive one such child as this in my name, receiveth me. And whosoever shall receive me, receiveth not me, but him that sent me. John answered him, saying: Master, we saw one casting out devils in thy name, who followeth not us, and we forbade him. But Jesus said: Do not forbid him. For there is no man that doth a miracle in my name, and can soon speak ill of me.*
    **Mark 9:32-38 (DRA)**

Then he flipped the pyramid over, and told John to beat his sword collection, born of the FUDS of OPML, which Zander & Zander call the "Calculating Self" in *The Art of Possibility*, into plow shares, and to use his Little Mustard Seed to plant a garden with whoever was of the same goodwill as **FOREVER.**

Jesus directed him to plant the garden together with these "others" by offering their Little Mustard Seed, born beyond themself from their common human heart, their "Central Self" as Zander & Zander posit. He said to simply let the garden grow, and give thanks to Alah for his super abundant Truth, and Beauty, and Goodness.

AND THEN… That's when Jesus took ALL of the air out of the FUDS of OPML for good as he followed up with…

- *For he that is not against you, is for you.*
    **Mark 9:39 (DRA)**

Read that again, just so you get the phrasing right.

Because Jesus knows a few things about our psyche, and what he has asked us to do, and what he asks us all to do even now: To be born again (or born from above), and, YES, Nicodemus, to pass again into Our Mother's Womb by the same fiat that allowed The Lord God of Hosts, The King of the Universe to pass into hers, and be born from above into this world as "bone of our bone, and flesh of our flesh", and, as the finishing touch on his Opus of Love, to offer up his flesh to us as the eternal food for our journey HOME to **FOREVER**.

This is the same pattern he uses for each, and every miracle he ever works, including my own entry into the Catholic Faith Tradition, the HOME that I shall never leave, and can always come back to even if I stray. I can come back by the virtue of my Baptism in The Name of The Father, and of The Son, and of The Holy Spirt… indeed in the name of **FOREVER,** where I literally spent some *Contact* time (ala Jodie Foster & The Tesseract Machine) with the Holy Trinity, and with Our Holy Mother of God on this most auspicious of days in my timeline [which has always been just a bit warped in a very good way ever since].

As I did earlier, I invite you to read the Mark 9:39 quote again, because like all things that Jesus said to turn us around, this saying gets us headed away from our Calculating Self, and thinking with the core of our common humanity, the pinnacle of creation here on earth, our Immanuel, our "Ellohim-with-Us", our "Mind of Christ" as St. Paul pens **(in [1 Corinthians 2:16](https://www.biblegateway.com/passage/?search=1+Corinthians+2%3A16&version=NRSV))**, that the self which the First Adam broke and left us all with an inheritance of our FUDS-laden Original Sin, and its residual concupiscence toward OPML thoughts, words, deeds, and omissions, that calculating, conniving, and other-suppressing self born of eternal death that Jesus, the "Second Adam" in his offering of his Death of Forever on a cross the fateful cross of Fear, Uncertainty, Doubt, Shame, and Sorrow ate, and swallowed up completely for us. In this case, what Jesus said literally reverses the whole course of human history, and makes as many as hear it, and act accordingly, into Peacemakers, rather than continuing to be the natural "Murderers in Broad Daylight" like Cain which we were "naturally" born of The Earth to be.

What you will hear, if you ignore your nativist, calculating flesh crying out, and listen with The Little Mustard Seed hidden in your heart of hearts in the very center of your Core Self, you will hear the exact opposite of what any despot, dictator, detractor, or spike-haired Dilbert of a boss has ever uttered to prod those "under them" forward as they sit inert on their puny little neurotic, Nimrod-esque pyramids **(cf [Genesis 10](https://www.biblegateway.com/passage/?search=Genesis+10&version=NRSV))** which they have built from the sand of a desert their nativist minds cannot escape.

You will NOT hear:

- *He who is not FOR me is AGAINST me.*

You WILL hear:

- *He who is <u>NOT AGAINST</u> y'all <u>IS FOR</u> y'all.*

And that reversal of NOT FOR IS AGAINST to NOT AGAINST IS FOR makes an Eternity of Difference, because your Eternal Life, and Our Ultimate Happiness Literally depend on it.

Yes it's binary, because, just like the judgement criteria of Matthew 25, and the command not to eat of The Tree of the Knowledge of Good, and Evil, and the root of every miracle Jesus has ever done here on Earth, and all things that Elohim has ever created, and all choices, which are each literally choices between life, and death…

IT'S ALL BINARY.

Just like every choice is truly a choice between eternal death, and eternal life, the choice between this pair of phrases is as well.

AND YET, THIS GETS EVEN BETTER!!!

By operation of The Agility of Grace, just like Elohim himself, the choice is "Trinary", because a choice for the Goodwill of "NOT AGAINST IS FOR", brings MORE than simply a selection between otherwise neutral options,.

The former self-limiting choice of "NOT FOR IS AGAINST", ONLY allows for an either-or option, requiring harsh FUDS to enforce the OPML thinking that drives its zero-sum function.

But the second choice of "NOT AGAINST IS FOR" allows for BOTH either-or, and both-and inclusion, which truly is who The Agility of Grace is as the Holy Spirit of the Holy TRINITY himself. To emphasize this nature, I repeated a phrase several times earlier in the Transilluminate Creed:

- ...by His Holy Grace, The Eternally Creative Golden Promise of The Eternal Community of The Ineffably Pure Light of Goodness & The Beautifully Pure Love of True Mercy, and...

The Agility of Grace ALWAYS stands BY, and, with His Grace, there is ALWAYS an AND, and HE, not "it" like some impersonal "force", is always standing BY us as The One, True Never-Ending Golden Creative Super-Abundant Fountain of Our Holy Grace whenever we are standing TOGETHER WITH him BY embracing his wisdom as the wisdom of The Original Holy Peacemaker of Mercy, the wisdom of the root of ALL Peacemakers, indeed the very wisdom of Peace as Mercy Himself (by the way the only place where righteous, and peace may kiss)...the literal PEACE of

**FOREVE!**

When we choose to EITHER stand together with him by embracing his GOODWILL, OR stand AGAINST him, by embracing the pitiful, death-inducing FUDS of OPML in the woefully limited context of our Calculating Selves, there is no "AND" anymore, there is only a single, solitary ME, and an OR NOBODY ELSE. This is the same ME OR NOBODY ELSE that Matthew 25 tells us will be left to rot forever without any GRACE at all, literally without any WATER at all to quench its thirst, this is the ME that will die an eternal death of self-loathing, and self-reprisal, and the infinite desolation of self-depredation in the NEVER-EVER with what *The Never Ending Story* directed by Wolfgang Petersen imagines for us as THE NOTHING.

And that's where Satan wants you to be as he drives you forward, and as he drive each, and every one of us apart from each, and every other with FUDS-born, OPML thinking... to a state of being completely divided, and alone forever (even if you are the only one there) where you shall literally be both "ME the PEOPLE" & "THE ENEMY OF THE PEOPLE" and THE NEVER NOTHING NEVER (as a god unto yourself alone, the unholy trinity of NEVER-EVER), with NO PATH OF ESCAPE, because The Agility of Grace will no longer be on offer for the goats of THE NEVER-NOTHING-EVER. Without demonstrating Mercy in your infinitesimally short life here on Earth, you will literally never have existed at all, because you will not have made an impact in the Universe, you will never have existed.

This is where Satan wants you to be, because this is where his rebellion against Elohim put both him, and his band of fallen angelic sycophants who shall continue to fall deeper, and deeper, and deeper into negative infinity, into the state of never have ever existing at all.

This is why they shall try until the End of Time to sow the seeds of discord, and, in grotesque futility, attempt to thwart The Agility of Grace that powers ALL Peacemakers EVERYWHERE, and gives even those who can't be bothered to be Peacemakers any of the good gifts that they may enjoy in the blink of an eye they enjoy here on Earth. And where do THEY, the never-caring, get the good things of the Universe? Literally from the hands of those who choose to be the Peacemakers of this world through their contributions of their cross-products of Mercy, even unto their own deaths:

- *You have heard that it hath been said, Thou shalt love thy neighbour, and hate thy enemy. But I say to you, Love your enemies: do good to them that hate you: and pray for them that persecute and calumniate you: That you may be the children of your Father who is in heaven, who maketh his sun to rise upon the good, and bad, and raineth upon the just and the unjust. For if you love them that love you, what reward shall you have? do not even the publicans this? And if you salute your brethren only, what do you more? do not also the heathens this? Be you therefore perfect, as also your heavenly Father is perfect*

    **Matthew 5:43-48 (DRA)**

It's not that Satan, whose name literally translates as "Our Accuser" as the full, and unnatural embodiment of MISERY loves your company, it's just that, like Cain, he doesn't want anyone else to have the GOOD THINGS of **FOREVER** from which he has been proscribed. It's not that he wants to party WITH you, it's that he wants you to party AGAINST YOURSELF, to be blinded by the neon of his false light, to forget your traveling companions in life, and to wind up so completely, and utterly alone, that you willfully commit Eternal Suicide in THE NOTHING NEVER EVER with *NO EXIT* which Sartre got almost right. Even the interaction is his play is more than a ME OR NOBODY ELSE person will ever never not exist enough to know in Hell.

Just ask anyone who has been in solitary confinement, BEING ALIONG truly is being in HELL.

You see, Sartre was almost right, only Hell is not "other people", Hell is the complete absence of anyone else, ever, the presence of the NO-ONE-ELSE-NEVER, and the COMPLETE ABSENCE of ALL GRACE that, from your perspective, never-ever didn't not exist in the infinitely void desert you have all to yourself by means of your never existing that you can never not be in, and therefore can never leave, because you are less than nowhere at all, and in a non-place, without even time as a fried, where you will never see nobody, nor nor nothing else of value, where you shall NEVER-BE INFINITELY LESS THAN NEVER NOTHING NOT-EVER.

Without MERCY, you will be an ever-imploding void of non-entity. You will NEVER BE NO NEVER FOR NONE OF NEVER.

You shall be…
***FORGOTEN!***

So the choice is always between being **FOREVER** in Eternal Love of Agility, and being THE NEVER NOTHING NEVER in your self-served Despairing FUDS of The Non-Existence of OPML as…
***THE FORGOTTEN!***

In contrast to being **THE FORGOTTEN** Air Supply has aptly crooned for us that The Agility of Grace is literally capable of rapturing us to a place we have never know, that is literally "like never before" teaching us how to Party for Mercy's Sake BY:

- *Making LOVE out of NOTHING AT ALL*

Taking our nativist destiny, and making us to:

BE-A-PEACEMAKER.COM

This is how, just like Elohim himself, by the Agility of His Holy Grace, we ourselves came to be. This is how we can be LIKE HIM. And just like him, we can do the seemingly impossible by creating a completely renewed universe EX NIHILO, whenever, and wherever we choose to plant The Garden of the Peacemaker, which is always as unique, and as wildly beautiful as the Peacemakers who make up the Peacemaking Enterprise who deigns to plant NOT AGAINST US.

This is why I invite you to throw your whole heart into being a Peacemaker at:

BE-A-PEACEMAKER.COM

I do this, because I know how steep the climb is to that Garden, and I know how impossible the passage is without the Catholic Faith Tradition, the Ancient Messianic Belief that began in that SAME Garden of Genisis 3:21, even before we were made to leave its paradise of…
***FOEVER!***

Even now, the Messianic conga continues in an unbroken line from Adam, to Able, and then to Seth, even into the hands of the local Parish Priest who continually offers you an open invitation to literally, physically, TOUCH GOD in this lifetime. YOU can receive this TOUCH of GOD in the real-and-present here-and-now, and to allow The Everliving Community of Love literally, truly, beautifully, physically, and with the perfection of perfect goodwill to

TOUCH YOU in the mysterious act of the Divine Intercourse of His Holy Grace (just as he did Mary of Nazareth, The Holy Mother of God), so that by his Agility, he might fecund your soul with Infinity, and help YOUR Little Mustard Seed to grow into its always intended Infinity, into a tree under which YOU & YOUR NEIGHBORS can literally become a childen again in the dancing arms of The Agility of Grace.

For this is the Pattern of Miracles that Jesus always used:

- *Engage someone with the intent to perform a miracle*
- *Introduce the idea to that person that* **FOREVER** *is possible, and the the PEACE of BEING* **FOREVER** *is at hand for the taking*
- *Ask the person who is to receive the miracle to do something impossible*
- *And then let the past experience of that person trigger the Little Mustard Seed within them to illuminate the dawn of the miracle of their faith, even if that resulted in letting that person continue in the way of their FUDS of OPML, even up to the point of blinding flashes on a road to nowhere leading to the murder of Faithful Peacekeepers of The Way of Mercy who had already found his miracle waiting for them in their own hearts, and who had already joined The Little Mustard Seed* **MERIPALOOZA FOREVER Corp…
FOREVER**.

Even in cases like the case of my own miracle of faith, which is a true testament to, and demonstrative proof of Mark 9:39, Jesus must allow you to go to the literal Throne Room of All Graces, and be dubbed a Knight of The Kingdom of God by Mary, Queen of the Universe, Mother of Mercy, and Queen of Grace herself, and then be left to TRY to be a Peacemaker FOR 29 YEARS without joining The Church he himself founded on St. Peter (Cephas [Κηφᾶς], meaning "The Rock" in Aramaic), and the unbroken line of the rest of the original Apostles that have kept her safe, and have kept safe the touch of he who is truly Our Manna Immanuel, "God With Us" as Elohim in the Flesh as a literal taste of **FOREVER** available in The Eucharist for us almost anytime we care enough to go find him (*cf* masstimes.org), even as he goes about Our Father's work of Divine Mercy, and stands ready beyond all time holding himself out to us as the Dodecahedral Tesseract of the Everyday Miracles of Peace, and invites us to Party with Him who is THE ORIGINAL MERCIPALOOZ.com for Mercy's Sake always Like Never Before, and always nourishes us with the ambrosia of his death eating flesh, so that we might literally eat of his FLESH OF **FOREVER**, and drink deeply of his life giving blood of human kindness, and then send us out to live life through that same Sang Real of MERCY which is truly the quest of ALL KNIGHTS of THE REALM, and truly the lifeblood of ALL Peacemakers of ALL TIMES, even until THE END OF TIME itself, and THE EXTINGUISHING OF THE FUDS OF OPML OF DEATH in…

**FOREVER.**

**Even in these truly unlikely cases such as mine, which honestly, we all are, the answer to The Question of the Peacemaker is a resounding "NO!"**

You don't have to be of the Catholic Faith Tradition to begin your labor of love for Mercy, but trying to do the miracle work of Mercy each, and every day will eventually catch up with you, and invite you in the door. And when you do take the invitation to TOUCH GOD & LET GOD TOUCH YOU, truly, physically, intimately, and infinitely in the real-and-present here-and-now, you will SEE the world in a whole new way, just as St. Paul did when the scales of forgiveness finally fell from his eyes on Straight Street.

Because if your are trying to work miracles by trying to be a perfect Peacemaker without the Eucharist, which is found ONLY in THE ONE HOLY CATHOLIC & APOSTOLIC CHRUCH, and if you are trying to Party for Mercy's Sake ALWAYS Like Never Before, without regularly experiencing the literal, truly, beautiful, physically present, perfectly practiced goodwill, and THE INFINITY OF THE TOUCH OF GOD by "pressing the flesh" and "shaking the divine hand" of Divine Mercy at the foot of Jacob's Ladder in the Embassy Mission of **FOREVER** which he has planted, and shall continue to franchise until THE END OF ALL TIME, and to plant ALL OVER THE GLOBE, then you are truly trying to push a wet rope up the hill of Calvary (you don't even have the luxury of the rock of Sisyphus). If you are making an honest best effort at pushing that rope, and then going out into the fields of the world to try to do The Perfect Work of The Peacemaker as a Perfect Opus of The Agility of Grace by offering up the flesh of your own heart, renewed daily by The Agility of Grace to be pressed out in both good times, and in sorrow, even unto the sorrow of death, should that be required of you, even as The Wine of The Human Kindness of Mercy delivered for The Ultimate Happiness of YOUR Neighbors, especially for those who are "the least of these", and perhaps "the least agreeable of these: who need your kindness the most" as the processes for becoming The Infinity of Happiness you were always meant to be…

Then at some point, especially if you have already been Baptized, but even if all you did was to cry out at birth, and let His Holy Grace pray with The Agility of Grace that Our Father in Heaven whose hallowed name is **FOREVER YOUNG** to plant the FOREVER CHILD of The Little Mustard Seed of Faith in your heart "with unspeakable groanings" (**Romans 8:26**), you will ask anew The Question of the Peacemaker of The Little Mustard Seed who lies within you, in your heart of hearts, and you will allow yourself to remember YOU into that **FOREVER YOUNG FOREVER CHILD OF FOREVER** again as you seek to remember again WHO YOU ARE: The Infinite Happiness You Were Always Meant TO BE. Then you will put down your sword of protest, seek the door to THE THRONE ROOM OF ALL GRACE, and run knocking on that very same door where you will find Jesus already, as Always Like Never Before, knocking for thee.

And then… We Shall Overcome, together, because you shall open that door, and drop your sword of protest at His feet, so that you may embrace Him with both hands, and sup WITH Him by supping OF Him, just as I did after 29 years of baptized life, and 50 years of mostly ignoring The Little Mustard Seed planted within my own heart by The Agility of The Holy Spirit of His Grace at my birth. And when you get back up off your knees, he shall hand you back your sword, transformed by His Grace into an Instrument of Peace, and you shall be a curious, and overworked Stranger of Grace no longer, because you shall now be joined WITH Him fully, as an Instrument of Peace in your shared Mother's hands, and his, and even the hand of The Holy Trinity of The Elohim of **FOREVER,** and even with me in fellowship, now with full-orbed faith.

You have begun to join The Full-fledged Ranks of the Peacemaker, as my fellow Knight, just by the act of picking up this book, and reading this far, because you have never been truly AGAINST me, or against the Jesus who turns all of the tables of the FUDS-Makers of OPML in this world upside-down enabling us, as The Peacemakers of **FOREVER** to move mountains from their strongholds, and fill up the valleys below them with the rubble, and make the crooked straight, and the rough places plain for Our Neighbors with Our Uniquely & Collaboratively Creative Noble Acts of Mercy offered up to them, and delivered to them through The Agility of Grace, so that we might help them find The Little Mustard Seed of The Peace Maker within themselves and lead them to that same Way of Mercy that miraculously carried us to them, which but for The Grace of God, we never would have been made to trod.

And then, as The Ever-Growing Ranks of The Peacemaker, basking in the warmth of The Ineffable Light of **FOREVER**, we shall walk on together, even through the ever-colder sea of those who are truly *against* us as they walk in strident strides of OPML opposition to both Jesus, and to us, on the way to their own, uniquely destructive, excruciatingly isolated, FUDS-laden eternity, even unto the time when ALL FLESH shall see together that same flash of Glory St. Paul saw on his way to Damascus.

AND that **FLASH OF FOREVER** shall put an end to ALL TIME, meaning that no Peacemaker shall ever be recruited again, for evermore.

YOU MAY BE FEELING "THE BURN OF THE PEACEMAKER" RIGHT NOW…

Even if it is the burn of the great anger you may feel toward me for being such a pompous ass, and for saying such things, and for being so binary, and so resolute in my grip on The Catholic Faith Tradition. You are feeling that burn, because your Little Mustard Seed really, really, really wants to come out, and play!

You really, really want Divine Intercourse with Elohim, right here, and right now, in the real-and-present here-and-now.

**DIVINE INTERCOURSE… It's what you want. It's what you really, really want!**

AND PERHAPS IT'S TIME…

..for you to stop playing with the wrong pieces in Pascal's Wager, and concede that perhaps, "Grant is not always wrong," and perhaps The Church which has existed from the very moment that Jesus gave Mary into Joh's care as one of the last seven words he spoke from the Cross of FOREVER.

If I AM right, and The Church is right, and you JOIN US at the Footstool of **FOREVER** at Mass in Worship of He Who WAS, and IS, and IS TO COME, then don't lose anything but the FUDS of OPML, and the pain that they are bringing you, and the time that they are robbing from you.

AND… You stand to **GAIN ETERNITY!**.

PERHAPS IT'S TIME…

FOR YOUR OWN FIAT of **MAGNIFICAT**.

PERHAPS IT's TIME…

FOR YOU:

*MY HEART MAGNIFIES THE LORD…*

TO ASK the Question of The Peacemaker
TO SEEK the Way of Mercy
TO GO to find that door your Little Mustard Seed of Faith is locked behind
(**cf MassTimes.com**)
TO KNOCK where He knocks for YOU
TO OPEN THE DOOR &
TO LET HIM OUT

**REGARDLESS OF:**
   **WHERE YOU HAVE COME FROM**
   **WHAT YOU HAVE LIVED THROUGH &**
   **WHAT POSITION YOU HAVE NOW TAKEN FOR YOURSELF ON YOUR JOURNEY**

BE-A-PEACEMAKER.COM — *SEEK FOREVER LOVE NOW!*

And join me in our shared journey of becoming the **FOREVER YOUNG FOREVER CHILDEN OF FOREVER**, which both of us were always meant to be, so that we may be adopted under the name, and grafted into The Holy Family Tree of…
**FOREVER**.

JOIN **The Little Mustard Seed** *MERCIPALOOZA FOREVER CORP* TODAY:

# BE-A-PEACEMAKER.COM

# The Plowshare of The Peacemaker

## The Rosary of Agility

For a full exposition on what this is, what to do with it, and how the Best Peacemakers get the most value out of this Sword-born, Grace-beaten, Mercy-blessed Plowshare pictured below, pick up my work entitled, *Be Mindful Little Mustard Seed* @ LMSSPT.com.

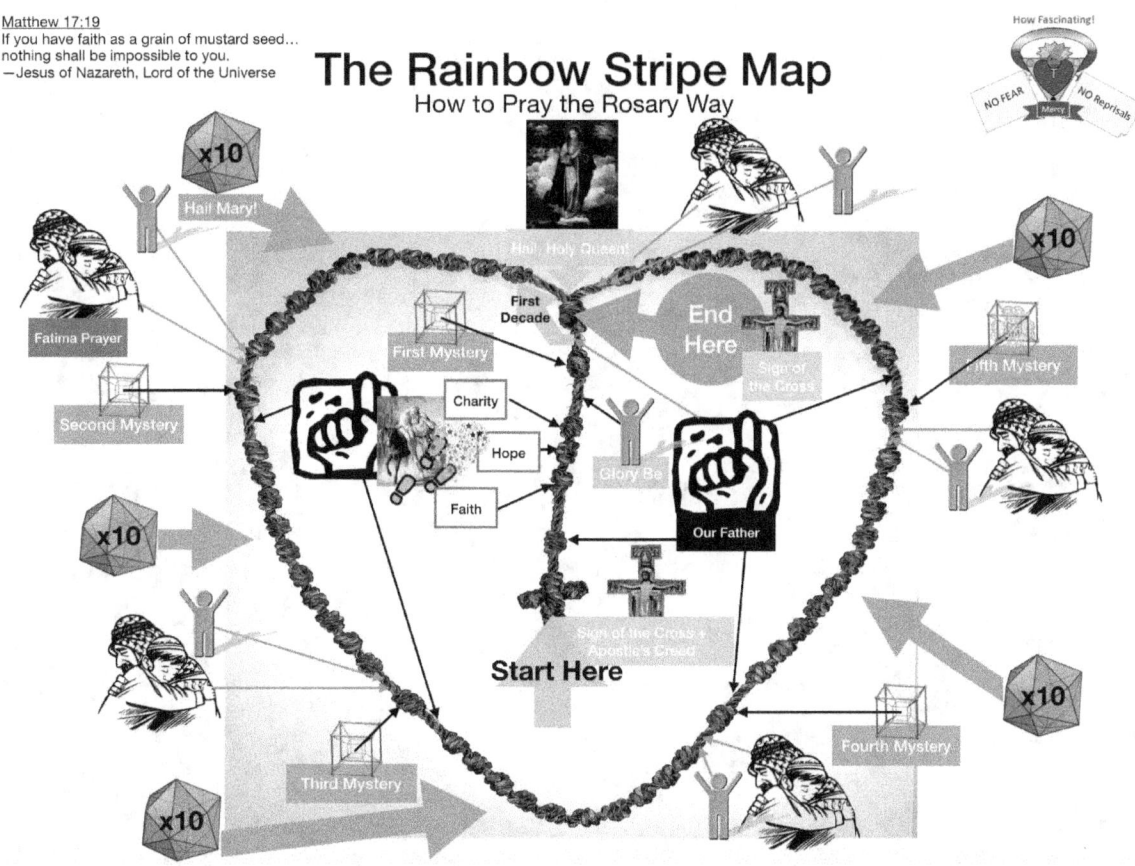

As for me… when I finally crossed over the transom into The Catholic Faith Tradition, and was able to eat the Eternal Ambrosia of God, the sword I had presented to Mary in The Throne Room of All Graces at my Baptism was finally transformed by The Agility of Grace… His Holy Grace of Her Right Hand… into a plowshare, indeed into an Instrument of Peace who I usually wear around my neck, so I always have Him at the ready to Wage Peace as my instrument of peace, resting in my right hand, resting in her left hand, even as she rests in the hand of her blessed son, Jesus, and even as He, The Christ as The Ultimate Instrument of Peace rests in the hands of The Agility of Grace, The Holy Spirit of The Holy Trinity of Elohim, The Eternal Community of The Eternal Love of MERCY, even as he rests upon The Throne of Our Father as Our Eternally King, and rests his feet for us upon the Altar of the Eucharist as himself, as MERCY TRANSUBSTANTIATED, Enduring…

**FOREVER!**

This is The Holy He who has chosen to specially prepare us, and to make us His Bride, His Holy She, whom through the plural-unity of our WE, and by His Grace of Collective Subsidiarity becomes the hands of His Body, literally of **His Little Mustard Seed MERCIPOALOOZA FOREVER CORP**, with His One & Only Little Mustard Seed of The Golden Creative Promise of **FOREVER** at the Sacred Headwaters of our great mustard tree, the very tap root of our gnarly, global grapevine that spans the eons. We are the extension of His Hands, which he stretches out as healing leaves through our hands, the hands we use every day to reach out to offer common, yet noble, and sometimes soul-crushing acts of Mercy to those who need The Agility of Grace more than we need them. We reach out from our He who crises out in thirst from His Holy Cross longing to touch them and to offer them the PURE Living Water of the wine of the His pinnacle of perfect human kindness, the ONLY drink worthy to quench the *Little Mustard Seed Fire* that has been lit by His Grace in their hearts. This is how He, through our Acts of The Agility of Grace, offers to them, and as Matthew 25 reminds us…back to himself… Ambrosia's companion Elixir of God-Inebriating Divine Love that, but for the crucifying death of The Holy Him, we would never be made to offer in praise of Him as His Holy Peacemaker Bride by lifting up our hands of helping hope to serve Our Neighbors as The Holy Hands of She Who Takes Our Life From Him, and Give It Back Again… in Glory…

**FOREVER**.

There is a "whole-nuther" book to be written on The Rosary of Agility, complete with Myers-Briggs integration to help you figure out where your particular personality type fits best in the web of the delivery backbone, and the prayer life guided by The Agility of Grace. These images will be in that book fully expounded, and published at LMSSPT.com as well (and they may even show up in *The Queen of Grace*, which is a Broadway-style Musical designed to reintroduce The Rosary back into common parlance well beyond the often too solemn walls of our church buildings). Until then, I offer you the least covered up version of her vignettes, and the Mystery Map to go with them to aid you in your prayers, which I **GUARANTEE YOU** will lead you to…
*FOREVER*.

|  | Χαιρε | **B** Mystery 1 | **I** Mystery 3 | **N** Mystery 5 | **G** Mystery 4 | **O** Mystery 2 |
|---|---|---|---|---|---|---|
| **GLORIOUS** | | The Resurrection of Jesus | The Provision of The Holy Spirit | The Crowning of Mary Queen of Heaven | The Assumption of Mary | The Ascension of Jesus |
| **SORROWFUL** | | The Bloody Prayer in The Garden | The Crown of Thorns | The Crucification of Jesus | The Enlistment of Simon of Cyrene | The Scourging at the Post |
| **LUMINOUS** | | The Baptism of Jesus | The Proclamation of The Kingdom of Heaven | HIS GRACE JOHN 3:16 The Institution of The Eucharist | The Transfiguration | The Wedding at Cana |
| **JOYFUL** | | The Annunciation | The Birth of Jesus | The Finding of Jesus in the Temple | The Presentation of Jesus at the Temple | The Visitation |
| **GLIMMERING** | | **Mercy is the Victory of Dignity:** AND Elohim Made for Them: Clothes | **LMS Mercipalooza Forever Corp:** The Laughter in The Law | **The Ineffable Light of Mercy Shines FOREVER** | **The Agility of Grace — Mercy Makes Us One:** Hiram's Help | **Mercy Trumps The FUDS of OPML:** The Just-Right Peace of Abram |

PEACEMAKERS ARE SERVANT LEADERS… FOREVER

# The Commission of The Peacemaker

## Matthew 28:18-20 (DRA)

**18** And Jesus coming, spoke to them, saying: All power is given to me in heaven and in earth.

**19** Going therefore, teach ye all nations; baptizing them in the name of the Father, and of the Son, and of the Holy Ghost.

**20** Teaching them to observe all things whatsoever I have commanded you *[which have literally been nothing but MERCY]*: and behold **I am with you all days**, even to the consummation of the world.

**Here Ends The Gospel of Matthew**

# The Hope of The Peacemaker

## To Overcome The FUDS of OPML & To Rest with Perfect Peace

- *To him that shall overcome, I will give to sit with me in my throne: as I also have overcome, and am set down with my Father in his throne.*
  **Revelation 3:21 (DRA)**

## The Invitation of The Peacemaker

### To Party for Mercy's Sake Like Never Before

- *I Jesus have sent my angel, to testify to you these things in the churches. I am the root and stock of David, the bright and morning star.* **And the spirit and the bride say: <u>Come</u>. And he that heareth, let him say: <u>Come</u>. And he that thirsteth, let him <u>come</u>: and he that will, let him <u>take the water of life, freely</u>.**
    **<u>Revelation 22:16-17 (DRA)</u>**

Come… Come… Come… LET US PARTY!

Let Us Take The Water of Life…

Freely…

BE-A-PEACEMAKER.COM

*FOREVER!*

## The Resolution of The Peacemaker

Therefore, Let Us Be Resolved:

To Go Forth sprinkling the MERCY-Dust of MERCIPALOOZA.COM everywhere we go, Baptizing Our Neighbors **BOTH IN THE WATER MADE REAL THAT MAKES US REAL** through the Sacrament of **THE BAPTISM OF *FOEVER*, AND IN THE BELIEF OF *FOREVER*** , The Holy Water of Life, The Holy Water of Our Unity Transformed By His Grace into Our Wine of Human Kindness, indeed, and in deed, in The Name of The Father, and in The Name of The Son, and in The Name of The Holy Spirit, teaching all those we meet To Party for Mercy's Sake Like Never Before, Even as Always Like Never Before, **WITH THE AGILITY OF GRACE**, so that we can Do More Better, To Be More Better, Even More Better, Each, and Every Day, and Make Our World a Better, Brighter Place **FOR US ALL** To Live In, and **TO LOVE IN**, until time shall tick, and tears shall drop…no more:

***FOREVER*!**

Because:

Your Eternal Life &

Our Ultimate Happiness

*Literally Depend on This…*

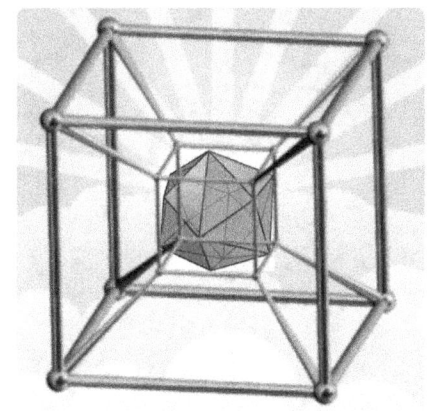

**YOU AND** Your Unending Charitable Work **Born Of Your Belief In Mercy, Who is JESUS,** The Christ, Our Brother;

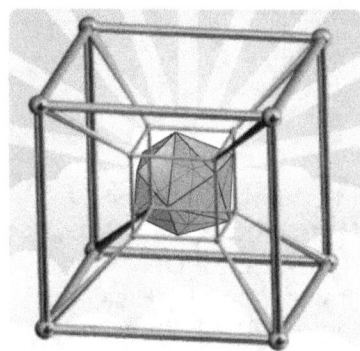

Who is
*The Least of These*,
Echoed
In Matthew 25
And
Present
With Us
Even
In THIS Moment
Of **THE DIVINE NOW**;

Who is
Both
Our Ultimate Judge &
Our Living Lord
Of Eternal Love;

**WHO IS
HIS MERCY
ENDURING**;

**WHO IS**...
*FOREVER*!

# The Haiku of The Peacemaker – The Sending Forth

Namaste!  Seek Love;

Serve Mercy:  Send Happiness;

Wage Peace:  *NAMASTE*!

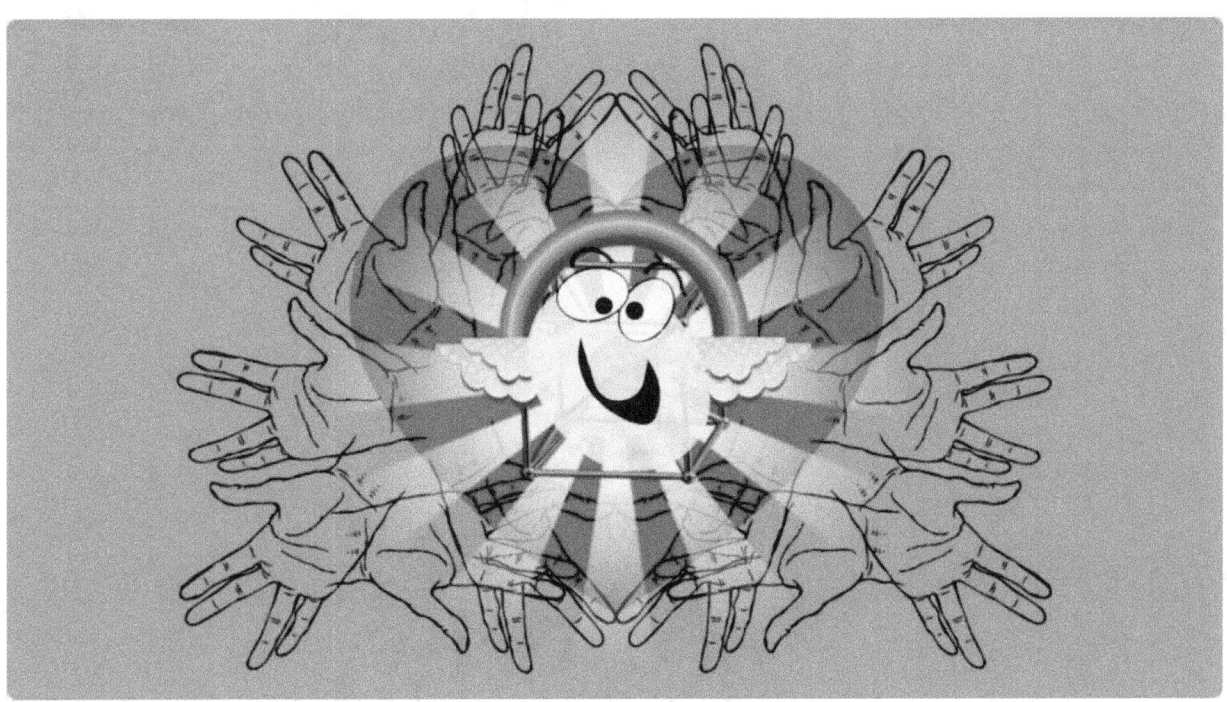

**The Beginning of the Peacemaker**

HERE ENDS YOUR SEARCH

FOR THE BEGINNING

OF YOUR

*FOREVER…*

BE-A-PEACEMAKER.COM

AND BE <u>ONE</u>

WITH…

*FOREVER*!

## The Dreams of the Peacemaker

IMPACT

As _____, a _____, I want to be able to deliver _____ to my Waiting & Thirsty Neighbors, so that _____!

## CONTRIBUTION

As _____, a _____, I want to be able to _____, so that _____!

ENGAGEMENT

As _____, a _____, I want to be able to _____ with _____, a _____ so that _____!

## DATA POINT

As _____, a _____, when I _____, I want to be able to sense _____ with my _____ in the form of _____, so that _____!

## TRANSCEND THAT BLOCKER – NAME IT & TAME IT

As _____, a _____, I am not able to _____ because _____!

**The Notes of the Peacemaker**

Write About What You Know…

www.ingramcontent.com/pod-product-compliance
Lightning Source LLC
Chambersburg PA
CBHW081442220526
45466CB00008B/2487